PUFFIN BOOKS

ERIC CANTONA

In its long and illustrious history, Manchester United has produced many footballing legends, from Duncan Edwards of the tragic 'Busby Babes', Bobby Charlton and Denis Law of the great 1968 European Cup-winning team, through to more recent heroes, like Bryan Robson and Ryan Giggs. But only George Best has been as idolized and held in such affection by the club's fans as Eric Cantona.

It is a love affair which began a long way from the din of another capacity crowd at Old Trafford, in a small town in France, where a young boy was swiftly marked out as possessing an unusual talent for football – and an ambition to match.

Eric Cantona

Fergus Kelly

PUFFIN BOOKS

*To Nikki – However many people are on the pitch,
I never want it to be all over.*

PUFFIN BOOKS

Published by the Penguin Group
Penguin Books Ltd, 27 Wrights Lane, London w8 5tz, England
Penguin Books USA Inc., 375 Hudson Street, New York, New York 10014, USA
Penguin Books Australia Ltd, Ringwood, Victoria, Australia
Penguin Books Canada Ltd, 10 Alcorn Avenue, Toronto, Ontario, Canada m4v 3b2
Penguin Books (NZ) Ltd, 182–190 Wairau Road, Auckland 10, New Zealand

Penguin Books Ltd, Registered Offices: Harmondsworth, Middlesex, England

First published 1996
1 3 5 7 9 10 8 6 4 2

Text copyright © Fergus Kelly, 1996
Photographs copyright © EMPICS Sports Photo Agency
All rights reserved

The moral right of the author has been asserted

Typeset in Monotype Baskerville by
Rowland Phototypesetting Ltd,
Bury St Edmunds, Suffolk
Printed in England by Clays Ltd, St Ives plc

Contents

Wembley Winner

LESS THAN FIVE MINUTES remained on the clock when the corner-kick swung across the penalty area. For the first time that afternoon, the Liverpool goalkeeper, David James, failed to catch the incoming ball cleanly with both hands. Instead, he succeeded only in punching it as far as the edge of the area, where it took a deflection, before dropping with a certain inevitability at one man's feet. He was instantly recognizable, and not just because of that upturned collar. The poise with which the player pivoted to strike the approaching ball in one flowing movement was unmistakable. So was the deadly accuracy with which he found the back of the net.

When the final whistle of the 1996 FA Cup final blew soon afterwards, Manchester United celebrated a unique achievement: the first club ever to win the Premiership and Cup Double twice. Their delighted fans were in no doubt who was chiefly responsible for this feat, and they chanted his name in salute around Wembley. On the pitch, he was being mobbed by his gleeful colleagues as their Liverpool opponents trudged off.

Eric Cantona did more than just score the winning goal that May afternoon. He crowned the most incredible comeback in football history. Only 16 months previously he had been banned from the sport in disgrace and barely avoided a prison sentence.

In the aftermath of the incident that night in January 1995 at Crystal Palace's ground, which shocked the whole country, nearly everyone involved with football was agreed, Eric Cantona was finished. No matter what the provocation he had suffered from an abusive spectator, it was felt that nothing could excuse the flying kick Eric had aimed at him.

The issue went as high as the House of Commons, with Members of Parliament calling for an example to be made of the player. Scathing newspaper headlines and stories adopted a similar tone, many demanding that he never be allowed to play in England again. Fellow professionals shook their heads sadly and said that Eric had gone too far this time.

The Football Association handed down an eight-month ban. Had it not been for an appeal by his lawyers, Eric would have gone to prison for two weeks. Instead, magistrates imposed a sentence of 120 hours of community service. There seemed no way back for one of the most gifted players to grace an English football pitch in the last ten years.

Yet, here he was now in 1996, not just scoring the winning goal, but captaining Manchester United to an astonishing second Double. As the team prepared to collect the FA Cup, Eric gestured to Steve Bruce to lead the players up to the royal box. Steve, who normally skippered the side, but had been forced to sit out the final through injury, smilingly refused. He knew as well as anyone the only person who deserved that honour.

At the bottom of the steps to the royal box there was one nasty moment. A small group of spectators lunged forward to spit at Eric as he passed them. It was a disgusting act and one which, not long ago, might have goaded the player into a violent response. Those who witnessed the moment held their breath. Staring briefly but contemptuously at his attackers, the Frenchman turned his back on them. Seconds later, he thrust the old trophy aloft, the first foreign captain to lift the FA Cup. The comeback was complete.

In its long and illustrious history, Manchester United has produced many footballing legends, from Duncan Edwards of the tragic 'Busby Babes', Bobby Charlton and Denis Law of the great 1968 European Cup-winning team, through to more recent heroes, like Bryan Robson and Ryan Giggs. But only George Best has been as idolized and held in such affection by the club's fans as Eric Cantona.

It is a love affair which began a long way from the din of another capacity crowd at Old Trafford, in a small town in France, where a young boy was swiftly marked out as possessing an unusual talent for football – and an ambition to match.

CHAPTER ONE

Le Brat

H E HAD BEATEN NEARLY every one of the opposing team's players on an amazing solo run, and seemed certain to score the goal which would make the score 1–1 – enough to add the league to the cup that his team had already won. Just as he was about to clinch that double, with only the goalkeeper to beat, the harsh blast of the whistle suddenly stopped him in his tracks. The boy looked up, stunned. He had done nothing wrong. But then he saw that the referee was pointing at his feet: he had been halted because his bootlaces were undone!

Even at the age of 12, Eric Cantona was already very difficult to stop. From the moment that his father, Albert, who had been a goalkeeper in his playing days, gave him his first football, the game became his passion. As a child, he would even wake in the middle of the night to check that his boots and kit had not been stolen. At a very early age, his family were agreed, young Eric was a natural.

Eric Daniel Pierre Cantona was born in Paris, on 24 May 1966. While he was still a baby, Eric's parents moved back to the family's hometown of Caillols, high in the hills above the city of Marseilles on the coast of the Mediterranean Sea. His grandparents, Joseph and Lucienne Cantona, had originally set up home there. They could not afford a normal house after they were married, so they moved into a cave in a hillside which during the Second World War had been used for a while as a lookout post by the occupying Nazis. The entrance was covered with a curtain. As Joseph was a stonemason he was soon able to build a house over the cave, which then became one of the bedrooms. By the time Eric's father and mother, Eleonore, moved back to Caillols, a second house had been built next door for them.

Eric was the second of three sons, and it was here, with brothers Jean-Marie and Joel, that he grew up, playing football on the family's patio. His great-aunt, Therese Morelli, recalls: 'The ball would always go over the wall and roll down the hill. He would make one out of paper and use that until someone returned it.'

His talent was quickly noticed and Eric was soon turning out for the local youth team, Sports Olympiques Caillolais. They built up a formidable reputation, losing only three or four times in more than 200 matches, and there was no doubt who was the star of the side. Yves Cicculo, the club president, later remembered how Eric joined the team while still at primary school. 'It was obvious from then, Eric was something special,' he said. 'He had all the qualities of a player. At nine, he was playing like a 15-year-old. When he was with us, we won lots of tournaments – and I can honestly say that he alone made the difference.'

Every Sunday, the entire Cantona family would come down from the hills to take their seats around the red-clay pitch, and watch Eric in action. Albert would urge him on from the touch-line. Former team-mates even remember his grand-mother, Lucienne, angrily shaking her parasol at opponents who had the nerve to bring him down.

Besides his obvious natural ability, Eric was also noted for his temperament. At the age of 13 he moved to the Grande Bastide school in Marseilles, after being chosen to do a special 'sports study' course, with an hour of football every day alongside normal lessons. In one report, prepared by the school for the French Football Federation in August 1979, he was described as 'emotive'. Next to the separate heading of Aggression was written one word: 'Active'.

According to one story from his schooldays, he is even reported to have been responsible for getting rid of the youth-team manager, who apparently resigned after the young Cantona, still only 13 years old, blamed him for a defeat. One of his teachers, Evelyne Lyon, recollected: 'I told him he'd better watch out, because talent was not enough, and if he didn't change his character he would have problems later. He was someone you always had to keep an eye on.'

It was during this time that Eric also gained the reputation as a loner which was to stick with him throughout his career. Caillols team-mate Christophe Galtier later recalled: 'We would be at the table eating, then Eric would go off to his room. He would stay there listening to music, or go to the cinema on his own. He had to be by himself. He never said why and we didn't ask.'

That streak of independence was evident when he left home, aged only 15, to begin his football career in Auxerre, 650 kilometres away. Word of this highly skilful youngster from near Marseilles had already spread around France. Auxerre was renowned as a club which specialized in nurturing young players, thanks to its manager, Guy Roux, who had taken the team from the French Fifth Division to become eventual First Division champions.

Guy Roux calls Eric 'the most brilliant of our youth trainees', and he still remembers the day that Eric started at the club in 1981. 'He came for training in May and joined us on 1 August.' Eric's mother and grandmother came to Auxerre to meet Roux and see how the youngster was settling in. 'I told them, he will play for France,' Roux says. 'He was like a matchstick, but he had class and he saw the game very clearly. He was always trying things. When they came off, it was magnificent – but often they didn't, and he gave the ball away. That was his principal fault. We had to teach him more discipline. He was mischievous, sometimes difficult, but children at that age are. There was nothing we couldn't deal with.' Roux's patience paid off. 'For the next three years with him, we won everything in junior football,' he says. The manager had learned early how to coax the most out of his new recruit. 'Eric always needs a father figure as his manager,' he said later. 'I had no problem with him. Eric does believe he's the best though, wherever he plays.'

It was not long before he was playing for Auxerre's first team. Eric made his professional début, aged 17, in November 1983 against Nancy. But, while Eric was developing into a highly promising young player, Roux was growing concerned that he kept disappearing every weekend to see his new girlfriend, Isabelle, in Martigues – which was nearly 600 kilometres away. 'Martigues had a club in the Second Division,' Roux says, 'and I told him to go there on loan. But he had to make up his mind. He had to return, with or without Isabelle. Five months later he was back – and married Isabelle.'

Eric's Auxerre team-mate Bernard Ferrer, who was Isabelle's brother, says that he had to be different even at the wedding. 'In our country you usually send out notices that you are getting married, but

Eric did it the other way round. He sent out the wedding announcements afterwards. That is typical of him.'

The goals, and the headlines about Auxerre's latest star, continued. At 21 years old, he played for France in their victory over West Germany, scoring on his international début. The following year he took part in the semi-final of the European Under-21 tournament, representing France against England. The French won the first leg at home 2–0. In the return game, at Arsenal's Highbury ground, a young English player called Paul Gascoigne caught the eye by putting England into the lead. But even he was overshadowed by Eric, who had scored both France's goals in what was eventually a 2–2 draw. It was the first time that two men who would so often be compared in the future had met on the pitch.

Eric was beginning to attract the interest of the biggest clubs in France, and people wondered how long Auxerre, which was not a particularly wealthy club, could hold on to him. In what was to be the first of many similar incidents, Eric provided the answer.

During a heated argument, he punched his team-mate and fellow French international, goalkeeper Bruno Martini, and was punished with a heavy fine by Auxerre. His days were clearly numbered. In June 1988 Eric made what looked like a dream move, to Marseille. He was not only back near his childhood home, he had also joined the best team in the country, and the high £2 million transfer fee – then a record in France – showed how much they valued him.

But the troubles which he largely brought upon himself would not go away. Not long after moving to Marseille, Eric was extremely abusive in public about the French national team manager, Henri Michel. As a result, he was banned from playing for France for a year. Things were not going much better at club level. He did not get on with Bernard Tapie, who was Marseille's multi-millionaire chairman and just as controversial as Eric.

In January 1989, during a charity match against Torpedo Moscow to raise funds for a Russian earthquake appeal, Eric was substituted. Infuriated by the decision, he kicked the ball into the jeering crowd, tore off his shirt and hurled it on to the turf. Marseille immediately suspended him, though he still won a championship medal with them that season – the first of many in both France and England. Then they loaned him to Bordeaux. By now, the French press had christened him 'Le Brat'.

Whatever the harm to his reputation, Eric's ability did not appear to suffer. He scored six goals in 11 appearances for Bordeaux, but he was soon on his way again, this time to Montpellier. He helped the club win the French Cup, scoring ten goals in 33 games, and it seemed that he had found somewhere he could settle. However, midway through the 1989/90 season, he was sacked. The reason, predictably, was another fight with a team-mate, after a dressing-room argument. He returned to Marseille.

This time, Eric was confident that he would be successful at Marseille. The club had appointed the legendary German Franz Beckenbauer as its manager. Beckenbauer had just led Germany to victory in the 1990 World Cup final against Argentina. He was the first man to perform the feat of winning the World Cup as both captain and coach of his country, having also played in the 1974 final, when Germany defeated Holland – a game Eric remembered watching on television as a young boy. He felt certain that Beckenbauer was someone who would bring out the best in him, and he looked forward eagerly to the new season.

Bad luck intervened. Eric injured his knee and was ruled out of the team, unable to make the good impression on Beckenbauer he had hoped. By the time he recovered, Beckenbauer had moved elsewhere, and had been succeeded by a Belgian coach, Raymond Goethals. Not for the first time – or, as it would turn out, the last – Eric did not see eye to eye with the person in charge of him. He later claimed that Goethals did not like the media attention Eric received. Eric was also still at odds with the chairman, Tapie.

His growing frustration at Marseille boiled over when he was named only as a substitute for a 1991 European Cup tie against AC Milan of Italy. It could only be a matter of time before he was on his travels again. That same year, after winning a second championship with Marseille, he was transferred to rivals Nîmes for £1 million. His new club named Eric as captain. But it was to be a short-lived responsibility. Only five months after signing for Nîmes, he was involved in the biggest controversy of his career yet.

Taking exception to a refereeing decision during a game against St Etienne, he reacted by picking up the ball and throwing it at the official's head. Before the referee had time to reach for the red card, Eric had accepted the inevitable, and was trudging towards the dressing-room. On the way, he got caught up in a fight with an opponent in the players' tunnel.

Four days later he found himself in front of a disciplinary hearing. The committee suspended Eric for four games. After the sentence was passed, the player was heard to mutter the word 'idiots'. Asked to repeat what he had just said, he walked up to each of the members of the committee in turn, repeating the word 'idiot' to their faces. They instantly doubled his ban.

Even so, no one, not even the French media, who had grown used to his outbursts, quite expected Le Brat's reaction to his sentence. At the age of 25, he announced that he was retiring from the game. The outcry that followed was extraordinary. The only other player anyone could remember voluntarily quitting the game so young was George Best (in whose footsteps Eric would eventually follow), when he retired from Manchester United, aged 26.

Eric's lawyer claimed his problem was that he was France's equivalent of Paul Gascoigne, saying: 'Everything he does is front-page news.' The mayor of Nîmes even begged him to change his mind. But he would not hear of it, branding everyone involved in the game in France 'a liar and a cheat'. He added: 'If French football doesn't want me, I don't want French football. Everyone seems to hate me.'

This was not true, of course. Among Eric's biggest admirers was the then manager of France, Michel Platini, who had been the country's greatest-ever player and one of Eric's idols. Platini had teamed Eric up front with Jean-Pierre Papin in what had become a high-scoring partnership. Eric alone had scored 14 goals in 20 internationals. With the 1992 European Championships in Sweden only six months away, Platini was anxious not to lose one of his most important team members. 'Eric is a player of talent and character,' he said. 'The French team needs players of character.'

Despite Eric's announcement, many clubs around the world showed an interest in signing him. Offers came in from as far away as Japan and Saudi Arabia. But Platini did not feel that the standard of football in such countries, which had only recently begun playing the sport, would be high enough. He believed the ideal move for Eric would be to

England, where he thought that his pace and strength would be perfectly suited.

Platini began contacting managers of English clubs to recommend Eric to them. Among those he telephoned was former England international Trevor Francis, then in charge at Sheffield Wednesday. Francis, himself noted for his ball skills during his playing days, liked what he heard. He became even more interested after speaking to Glenn Hoddle, who at that time was managing Swindon Town. Previous to that, Hoddle had played in the French league with Monaco, and knew all about Eric. 'If you get the chance, go and get him,' he told Francis. Not long afterwards Eric Cantona said goodbye to France and crossed the English Channel.

CHAPTER TWO

Ooo-Aah, Cantona!

THE RECORD OF FRENCH players who had previously come to England was not exactly a long and glorious one. In fact, before Eric Cantona, only two of them had made a similar journey: Didier Six, who played in a handful of games for Aston Villa in the Seventies, and the even more obscure Ollie Bernardeau, who had turned out for lowly Chesterfield in the mid-Eighties. Both had rapidly disappeared.

So, when Eric was presented at a press conference at Sheffield Wednesday's ground, Hillsborough, in January 1992, there was no great excitement about his arrival. There was, however, a lot of curiosity about a player who had captured so many headlines in France. Wednesday's manager, Trevor Francis, was well aware of the reputation that Eric had gained. 'Eric is their equivalent of Paul Gascoigne. In the French newspapers he's front-page news like Gazza,' he said. 'We've had a host of French journalists and radio reporters at Hillsborough wanting to talk about him to everybody, right down to our tea lady.' The manager also revealed that, in their telephone conversations, Michel Platini had likened Eric to Holland's deadly striker Marco van Basten. 'He said Eric's as gifted as the Dutch star and has the same eye for goal,' Francis claimed.

Despite Platini's recommendation, though, Wednesday had not signed Eric. Instead, the club had agreed to give him a week's trial, with a view to buying him permanently, or at least until the end of the season, from Nîmes. The transfer fee discussed was £750,000 – which looked like a bargain for someone of Eric's ability, especially considering the amounts that he had previously cost.

It was obvious that Eric saw the move to England as an opportunity to forget his past. 'I intend to leave behind all the problems I've had in France,' he told reporters, speaking through an interpreter. 'I believe my move into English football will allow me the room to breathe a little. I certainly hope there will be no trouble while I am with Sheffield.' He added that he knew how most people regarded him, and protested: 'Whatever I do back home is immediately all over the papers. But I'm not a bad boy.'

Whatever else he was, Eric was clearly not what people thought of as a typical footballer. For one thing, not many of his playing colleagues would list writing poetry among their hobbies. Yet Eric was well known in his own country for creating his own verse. Not long after arriving in England, he revealed that one of his heroes was the famous French poet of the 1800s, Arthur Rimbaud. As it is pronounced the same, many people at first thought he was referring to Rambo, the film character played by Sylvester Stallone!

Eric's other passions were painting and motor-bikes. His love of art was planted in him by his father, who had a studio in their Caillols home, where Eric learned to paint. Sitting in front of an easel is still one of his favourite ways of relaxing, and he often donates his work to be auctioned for charity. Riding motorbikes, especially Harley-Davidsons, on which he has been pictured looking like another of his heroes, film-star Mickey Rourke, is another way he gets away from it all.

Unfortunately, for both Eric and Sheffield Wed-nesday, his first visit to England coincided with the most bitterly cold week of the winter so far. The club's training pitch froze over, and the only chances that Francis got to see Eric in action were on arti-ficial or indoor surfaces. Not content with such a limited viewing, the Wednesday manager told the Frenchman that he wanted to extend his trial until he had seen him perform on natural grass. Eric was deeply offended. Refusing Francis's terms, he sent a fax, after speaking to his lawyer, which read: 'I've enjoyed my stay in England. But I don't wish to have a second trial and now I am going home. Thanks.'

Francis was surprised by Eric's response. 'I wanted Eric to stay on trial for another week. That request has been rejected and he has gone back to France,' he said. 'I am disappointed that Cantona and his lawyer did not regard my request as reasonable. He and his lawyer told me that he is a big star in France and would lose face with the people there if he stayed for another week on trial. But I have to do what I think is right for Sheffield Wednesday.' Francis added: 'I think that even the greatest manager in the world would not have been able to make a decision on a player after seeing him in two training sessions on an artificial pitch and one indoors.' It seemed as though Eric's career in England was over before it had even started. Then, Howard Wilkinson, the manager of Wednesday's Yorkshire neighbours Leeds United, got in touch.

In the late Sixties and early Seventies, Leeds had been one of the most successful clubs in the country, with a team that included such household names as Jack Charlton, Billy Bremner, Johnny Giles, Allan Clarke and Peter Lorimer. Managed by Don Revie, Leeds won two League Championships, the FA Cup, the League Cup and the European Fairs' Cup (which would later become known as the UEFA Cup). But, when Revie departed to take the England manager's job in 1974, the team began a slow but steady decline, even though it did reach the 1975 European Cup final, losing 2–0 to German champions Bayern Munich.

A succession of managers, including former playing favourite Clarke, failed to reverse the slump in Leeds' fortunes and, in 1982, the side was relegated from the old First Division. For a club the size of Leeds, which had won so many honours, it was a shattering blow. Nor did it bounce straight back. For eight years, Leeds struggled to regain anything like their former status, and seemed condemned to be regarded as a once-great club with little prospect of enjoying the good times again.

Wilkinson, however, had started to restore the club to its former glories. The outlook could not have been much worse when he arrived as manager, in October 1988. Leeds were second from the bottom of the old Second Division, and the club's shrinking number of supporters were starting to fear what would have been unthinkable a little earlier: relegation to the Third Division.

Confidence grew quickly under Wilkinson and Leeds avoided the dreaded drop. The following season they made their promotion intentions plain early on and always looked likely candidates to return finally to the First Division. Perhaps their manager's shrewdest signing was Gordon Strachan, whom he bought for a bargain £300,000 from Manchester United, and immediately made captain. Strachan led by example, and was ably supported by another, perhaps more surprising, purchase.

Vinny Jones came to Elland Road with a notorious 'hard man' reputation which had seen him booked and sent off more than most during his career. But Wilkinson saw him as exactly the sort of player required in the tough slog to get Leeds out of the Second Division, and Jones proved his value, rapidly becoming a favourite of the fans. His signing was also an example of how Wilkinson was not afraid to work with players who were meant to be difficult, something he was about to repeat with a certain Frenchman.

In 1990, Leeds were promoted to the First Division, a mere 18 months after Wilkinson took charge of the team. Now, in only their second season back in the top flight, they were challenging strongly for the Championship, in what was becoming a two-horse race with Manchester United. The modern team looked set to bring Leeds its first honours since the Revie years. Strachan was again playing some of the best football of his career, supported by the likes of Scottish midfield international Gary McAllister, much travelled forward Lee Chapman, and flying winger Rod Wallace, alongside such highly promising young players as David Batty and Gary Speed.

At first sight, Eric did not seem to be the type of player who would appeal to Wilkinson, a quiet and serious Yorkshireman who appeared to be the exact opposite of the emotional and passionate Frenchman. But, after having Eric recommended by Lawrie McMenemy (then England's assistant manager) and telephoning both Glenn Hoddle and

French boss Platini for their advice, Wilkinson made his offer.

Wilkinson also much needed another forward, as first-choice striker Chapman was out of action after breaking a wrist in the side's FA Cup third-round defeat by Manchester United. Eric was delighted to accept another opportunity to play in the First Division, and Leeds paid Nîmes £100,000 to take him on loan for the rest of the season, with the promise of another £900,000 to come if they then bought him permanently.

This time there were no hitches. Eric proved an instant hit in training with his admiring new teammates. One of them, David Batty, commented: 'Eric is the sort of player who can make fools of defenders if they try to niggle him. For a big man he has tremendous skill. He's impressed us all in training.' Batty added: 'He seems determined to live down his reputation. He desperately wants to make the most of his chance in English football.' Auxerre manager Guy Roux, who had been following his former pupil's progress, agreed: 'Eric will want so badly to play in the European Championships for France that he won't let anything bother him. A lot has been said about him, but deep down he's a nice boy,' he claimed.

Hoddle, the man who had first recommended Eric to Trevor Francis, had little doubt that Eric could make his mark in the English league, but he expressed concern about his temperament: 'I don't believe there are any worries over Eric's ability to handle the physical side of our game. He knows how to put himself about, too. The only question mark I'd put against him is whether the pace of the English game might be too frenzied for him. If he can settle quickly, he'll be a great asset for Leeds.'

He was an asset who began his Leeds career on Saturday 8 February 1992 at Boundary Park, Oldham. The media interest beforehand was enormous, and the team could hardly get out of the dressing-room because there were so many reporters and cameramen crammed into the tunnel to see the French newcomer. And this even though the object of their attention was not in the starting line-up. Wilkinson was wary of playing Eric from the opening whistle, not just because he had been out of first-team football for two months since announcing his retirement in France, but also because he wanted to let Eric get used gradually to the rough and tumble of the English game.

So, it was not until well into the second half that he was brought on to replace Steve Hodge, to a huge cheer from the travelling Leeds fans. The pace of the game was faster than anything he had been used to in France, and there was the added problem that the rest of the team had chosen Eric's début to turn in their worst performance for a long time. They were 1–0 behind when he came on, and three minutes from the end conceded a second. It was only the second defeat that Leeds had suffered in

28 League games that season. While he had little opportunity to impress, Eric was still able to show some of the delightful touches which would swiftly make him a hero among the club's supporters.

Eleven days later Eric was named in the French team to play England in a friendly at Wembley. It was seen as an important warm-up for both countries, with the European Championships moving ever closer. Some members of the French football authorities were not keen to see Eric in the side, because of his less than shining discipline record before he had left to join Leeds.

However, Platini threatened to resign as manager if his selection was opposed: 'If they try to put any pressure on me regarding Eric or any other player, I will leave the job.' Eric was included in the team, but hardly set Wembley alight with his brilliance. Neither did the rest of his French team-mates, and they slumped to a 2–0 defeat, in a game which was notable for Alan Shearer scoring on his England début and Gary Lineker hitting his 47th international goal, to take him within two of Bobby Charlton's record of 49 – a record which, sadly of course, Linker was not to beat. Eric managed one shot on goal after five minutes, which came off a defender and was cleared. After that, he barely figured in the action again.

Ron Atkinson, then in charge of Aston Villa, was among those who were convinced that, despite this poor performance, Eric had massive potential to be successful in the English league. When Villa met Leeds at the start of the following month, Eric again came off the bench and impressed everyone watching, even though he did not break the deadlock in the game, which finished 0–0. Praising Wilkinson's decision not to pick Eric from the start, Atkinson claimed: 'Howard's playing it exactly right with big Eric at the moment. The dilemma for him is slotting a very talented player in at a crunch period for his team. Sitting him on the bench and employing him when the rest are tired late in the game is perfect. I worried about Cantona when I saw him against England. I wondered if he could come to terms with the tempo of our game. But he has pace and he's sorting it out. Give him a few more weeks and he could have cracked it. By the time we get to the final month of the season he could have tuned in and be a revelation.' Atkinson would prove to be a shrewd judge.

At the beginning of March, Leeds underlined their determination to win the Championship with a 3–1 demolition of Tottenham Hotspur at White Hart Lane. Eric was brought on in the 76th minute, after receiving a deafening roar from the travelling supporters – just for warming up! Within a minute, he laid on a stunning pass for McAllister to score the third and decisive goal. Eric revealed afterwards that he had been moved by the way he was greeted. 'The reception was unbelievable,' he gasped. 'No one in France gets that sort of cheer just for running up and down the touch-line. I was so proud because some of my family came over to watch the game – my dad, Albert, and brothers, Joel and Jean-Marie. All the players at Leeds have helped me to settle in. I don't speak much English and they don't speak much French, but football is a global language. We sort out any problems with our hands, rather than our mouths.'

It was becoming increasingly evident that Eric was forming an understanding with Chapman up front. In his first full home game at Elland Road, Leeds routed Wimbledon 5−1. Chapman grabbed a hat trick and Eric scored his first goal for Leeds. But most Leeds fans would pinpoint the afternoon of Saturday 11 April, in a home game against Chelsea, as the moment when they really took Eric to their hearts.

Once more he had come on as substitute in the second half. He had been on the field only six minutes when he received the ball on the right, on the edge of the Chelsea penalty area. Cutting in, Eric outrageously flicked the ball, not once, but twice, over the head of approaching defender Paul Elliott. Then, still juggling the ball in mid-air, he unleashed an unstoppable volley past helpless goalkeeper Dave Beasant into the top corner of the net. The Leeds fans erupted, not quite able to believe what they had just witnessed. Nor could defender Elliott. He admitted after the game: 'You have to applaud ability like that. It was just quality and so is he. Very, very talented. His goal was simply marvellous.' Elliott, who had previously played alongside some of the best players in the world during a spell in the Italian Serie A with Pisa, added: 'I can honestly say that I haven't seen anything like it since I was playing in Italy – and then it came from Marco van Basten. That should tell you everything.'

Leeds captain Strachan was similarly lost in admiration, saying: 'OK, it suited Eric to come on late when all the wham-bam stuff was out of the way. That was the perfect stage for him to take over. But he took his chance brilliantly. It was the sort of goal I'll be telling people about when I'm 65. Surely that finish was worth the admission money on its own. I have seen thousands of goals and that was as good as any – right up there with all the truly memorable strikes.'

Leeds ran out easy 3–0 winners, and Eric laid on a goal for Chapman just for good measure. He had truly arrived, and it was around this time that the now familiar chant of 'Ooh-Aah, Cantona!' was born. Soon it was reverberating around Elland Road and every League ground that Leeds visited. Even the old Leeds song 'Marching on Together' was adapted to '*Marchons Ensembles*' to make the new boy feel at home.

The Championship remained a desperately close-run affair. The week after that Chelsea game, Manchester United remained favourites to win. They were two points ahead of Leeds and also had a game in hand. But the Frenchman seemed to give Leeds an added edge. He came on as sub for the last 15 minutes of a midweek game against Coventry City and had a shot stopped on the line by a defender's hand ball. From the resulting penalty, McAllister clinched a 2–0 victory. On the same night, Manchester United stumbled badly, losing 2–1 at home to Nottingham Forest. The Leeds fans were certain that Eric was their lucky charm.

The man himself was overwhelmed by the reception he was given at his new home. 'Everywhere I've been, people have made me feel very welcome,' he said. 'I didn't know of Yorkshire people's reputation for being cold and blunt before I came here and, having mingled with them and met them, my experience has been exactly the opposite. It only goes to show that reputations can be misleading. I have a reputation of my own – of being the bad boy of French football – but look at me now.' Eric also made it clear that he had no intention of ever returning to play in the French League again. 'In just two months in England I feel more at home than I ever did in France. Now that I have mastered the perils of driving on the wrong side of the road, I can cope with anything!' While there was still some uncertainty over whether or not Leeds would sign Eric permanently at the end of the season, he was certain about what he wanted to do: 'There are still a few details to iron out. But I want to stay and Leeds want me to stay,' he said.

The reason for the remaining uncertainty was the fact that Eric's appearances were still mostly as a substitute. He appeared in 15 games in that 1991/92 season, scoring three goals. But he started on only six occasions. Eric had become a 'super-sub' for Leeds, someone who came on late in the game and then turned it in Leeds' favour with one moment of magic or a vital goal. Howard Wilkinson made no apologies for often not playing him for the full 90 minutes. 'Being left out of the starting line-up might be a reason for protest in France,' he said, recalling Eric's troubled time at Marseille and other clubs. 'But Eric realizes there are players better equipped to deal with the English First Division than he is at the moment. What Eric really needs is the benefit of having a full pre-season of English training under his belt.' Though no one knew it at the time, here were the roots of a problem which would later cause Eric and Leeds to go their separate ways.

For the moment, however, nothing could spoil Leeds' dash for the Championship. The title was sealed on Saturday 25 April when Manchester United lost 2–0 at Liverpool and Leeds came from behind to win at Sheffield United 3–2. Eric never got further than playing as substitute for each of the team's last five fixtures that season, but that was of little concern to the adoring fans. His team-mates, too, recognized the difference he had made to Leeds' performances. As Lee Chapman said: 'Eric's ability to run at players and create situations out of nothing has encouraged those around him to be more adventurous.'

The fact that the club had won its first League Championship in 18 years was reason enough for celebration. The fact that by doing so they had foiled their biggest rivals' hopes of winning the title for the first time in a quarter of a century made the triumph even sweeter. There was disbelief at Old Trafford that the trophy they wanted to win above all others had slipped through their fingers again. Manager Alex Ferguson vowed that the club would be back to win it the next year.

At a civic reception thrown by Leeds Council to salute the team's success, Eric, who still spoke little English, went out on to the balcony of the city hall. Looking down at the thousands of people who had crowded the streets, he said: 'I don't know why I love you, but I do,' and got the biggest cheer of the day.

Not surprisingly, Leeds paid Nîmes the £900,000 that the two clubs had earlier agreed to complete Eric's transfer. In less than six months, he had gone from turning his back on football in his home country to becoming one of the hottest properties in the new FA Premiership, which was to begin the following season. That summer he went to Sweden to play for France in the European Championships, with high hopes. 'I'm proud to be French and want us to win,' he declared. 'And if we do, it would crown a season that was becoming a nightmare.'

The French were placed in the same group as England – and had an equally disappointing tournament. The two countries played out a spectacularly dull 0–0 draw in their clash in Malmo. While Eric hardly got a kick, he was far from being the only player in that game who wanted to put it behind him as soon as possible. Like England, France failed to get beyond the group stage, with hosts Sweden and eventual winners Denmark going through instead. Not much later, Eric's old friend and big influence Platini resigned as the French manager.

Eric was back to his sparkling best two months later at Wembley. Leeds were playing in the FA Charity Shield, the traditional opening fixture of a new season, between the previous season's champions and FA Cup winners – on this occasion, Liverpool. Picked to play from the start, Eric did more than justify Wilkinson's confidence in him, putting Leeds ahead after 26 minutes when he fired home a cross from Rod Wallace. Although Ian Rush equalized eight minutes later, Tony Dorigo restored the lead just before half-time.

But it was in the second half that Eric really took over the show. After Liverpool had pulled the score back to 2–2, he struck again with a right-foot drive and then, with three minutes remaining, he headed his third goal and settled the result, even though Liverpool managed one more goal in the final minute. It was the first hat trick in the history of the

Charity Shield, and the start of Eric's knack of scoring important goals at Wembley.

He said afterwards: 'I'm overwhelmed. I can't express what it means to a Frenchman to play in front of such a crowd, against Liverpool, and win. But I still feel I haven't arrived and still have to prove myself every week.' Wilkinson, meanwhile, was winning lots of praise for taking the risk of buying Eric in the first place. 'Eric was always the sort of player that you would step back from signing. I knew that and people kept telling me *"non, non, non"* when I was looking at him,' the Leeds manager recalled. 'They said you couldn't trust him. They might be right yet. But he had ability. It was an ability that struck you between the eyes. I had been in the game 20 years and in that time I have seen a lot of footballers, but probably only Glenn Hoddle and John Barnes, that I have dealt with, have as much talent as Eric.'

The Leeds fans echoed everything Wilkinson said about Eric, and more. To them, he could do no wrong. A record was released by a local band in the Frenchman's honour, called – what else? – 'Ooh-Aah, Cantona', featuring the now familiar supporters' chant mixed into a dance track. Gordon Strachan claimed: 'He is already the idol of Leeds, a legend in six months.'

Little more than a fortnight after his Charity Shield hat trick at Wembley, Eric cracked another one, this time at home to Tottenham Hotspur in the Premiership. 'French Lesson!' screamed the newspaper headlines, and they were not wrong. Eric dominated the 5–0 victory with his lethal finishing, his goals coming in a row after Wallace had opened the scoring. He should have had four, but when he looked certain to claim another one, he unselfishly passed at the last moment to Chapman, who completed the massacre.

Wilkinson paid tribute to Eric's latest performance, but once more he seemed to suggest that he was not entirely satisfied with his French star. 'Eric is still coming to terms with our football. Hopefully he will make the transformation complete soon,' he commented. 'There is still more to come from him. I feel he is still fitting in a bit and getting used to the pace of our football. Of course, he is more at home now, knowing things are a little quicker in this country. At times last season he wasn't able to get a kick.'

A much bigger clue that all was not well behind the scenes between the manager and Eric lay in Wilkinson's autobiography, which came out at around this time. He admitted that the Frenchman had made an immediate impression on the club, writing: 'After just two or three days in training, I knew we were witnessing a player of special natural talents.' But he pointed out that the Championship triumph had been achieved after he took the decision that Eric should not start most games. 'From then on his limited, but crucial, role would be that of a substitute,' Wilkinson said. 'I knew his virtuosity and flair would flower better in the last 30 minutes, when opponents had lost their bite.' What was perhaps even more surprising was that Wilkinson had apparently not changed his opinion of Eric in the new season, even though he scored 11 goals in 19 games. For Wilkinson claimed: 'The big question now is whether Eric can adapt his outstanding ability to the helter-skelter of our game. We still don't know, but if you scrutinize the evidence you have to admit his chances are less than even.' What the manager was saying was that he thought it was more likely that Eric would fail than succeed in English football.

While Leeds' supporters remained blissfully unaware of the fact, those words from Wilkinson's book were the clearest evidence yet that their hero might not be at Elland Road much longer. Little did they know how quickly he would be gone. Even worse, he would be going to their biggest rivals.

CHAPTER THREE

Red Devil

THE TELEPHONE RANG ON Manchester United Chairman Martin Edwards's desk as he was talking to manager Alex Ferguson. It was the Leeds United Chief Executive, Bill Fotherby. The two men were often in touch with each other. But this time, Fotherby was calling for a particular reason. He wanted to know if United were willing to consider selling their Republic of Ireland international full-back, Denis Irwin. The answer was immediate. 'Come off it,' Edwards said, insisting that the Irishman was not for sale at any price. Ferguson, listening to the conversation, whispered across the desk: 'Ask about Cantona.' Edwards did not hear what his manager said, so Ferguson scribbled Eric's name down on a piece of paper and passed it to the chairman. 'What are the chances of you letting us have Eric Cantona?' he asked. To his surprise, Fotherby made it clear that such a move might be possible, and rang Howard Wilkinson on his carphone.

Wilkinson, who was picking up his son from school, sat in his car and weighed up the United offer which Fotherby had told him about. Only a few days before, Eric had demanded a transfer after being left out of the team to face Arsenal in the Premiership. He said he wanted to stay in England, and named Liverpool, Arsenal and Manchester United as clubs he was willing to join. Wilkinson, aware that Eric had walked out on previous clubs, later recalled: 'I could see Leeds being the latest in line. We would have been left without our player and without a penny.' United were prepared to pay £1.1 million for Eric. The Leeds manager made up his mind. 'OK, do it,' he told Fotherby.

United were informed that, for the agreed fee, Eric Cantona was their man. With the deal completed, Ferguson contacted his assistant manager, Brian Kidd, and asked him if he would like to see Eric playing for United. Kidd naturally said yes. Told that the Frenchman was on his way to Old Trafford and what he cost, he gasped: 'For that money? Has he lost a leg or something?'

As news of the deal became public, the reaction in Leeds was one of even greater shock and disbelief. Fans jammed the switchboard at the local radio station, stunned by his departure, and horrified to discover where he was going. 'Anywhere but there' was the most common refrain. While the move came as a surprise to the supporters, it had been on the cards for some time.

The bright start that Leeds had made to the 1992/93 season – such as the Charity Shield victory over Liverpool and the defeat of Tottenham which featured Eric's hat trick – was not maintained. As the club's form dipped, Eric once more found himself left out of the starting line-up and grew increasingly frustrated. Not that this did anything to dent his popularity. In September, when the team flew to Germany to face Stuttgart in the first round of the European Cup, they were waved off at the airport by signs which read: '*Bonne Chance*' – 'Good Luck'.

On the night, Leeds' luck was out, however. They conceded three goals in the space of 19 minutes in the second half, the first coming when Eric gave the ball away in his own half. To make matters worse, he then hobbled off with a muscle strain. Leeds could not manage even a solitary goal in reply. Their chances of proceeding any further in the competition were written off by the press.

Yet, in the return leg a fortnight later, Leeds – and Eric – turned in an incredible performance. They thrashed the Germans 4–1. Eric combined with Strachan to set up Gary Speed for the first goal after only eight minutes. After McAllister extended the lead with a penalty, Eric produced a superb strike to put Leeds three up. Taking a pass from Strachan, he held off defenders challenging him on either side, and then lobbed the goalkeeper with a beautifully judged shot.

Sadly, Stuttgart did manage to score once, and that away goal counted double in the final 4–4 aggregate result, to send them into the next round. But there was more drama to come. It was revealed that the German club had broken the tournament's rules by fielding four foreign-born players, one more than permitted. Instead of being kicked out of the Cup as expected though, Stuttgart were ordered to replay the tie with Leeds, this time on a neutral ground.

The two teams met at the giant Nou Camp Stadium, home of Spanish club Barcelona, on 9 October 1992, and Leeds won 2–1. Their reward was a second-round clash with reigning Scottish champions, Glasgow Rangers, which was instantly dubbed 'The Battle of Britain'.

In the first leg, at Rangers' home, Ibrox Park, Leeds were beaten 2–1, and Eric had an extremely quiet game. He was left out of the team in the following league game, a 2–1 defeat by Queen's Park Rangers, and although he came back for the 2–2 draw with Coventry City, Eric again rarely figured in the action. Even so, he was named in the team for the second leg of the European Cup tie against Rangers, at Elland Road.

Five minutes into the game, Eric almost scored, with a lob which beat the goalkeeper, Scottish international Andy Goram, but it was cleared off the line by a defender. Almost immediately, Rangers went upfield and Mark Hateley headed them into the lead. It was a blow from which Leeds did not recover, and after 59 minutes, Ally McCoist made certain that the Scots would win with a second goal. Despite Eric's best efforts – a fierce shot which Goram turned away and a consolation goal five minutes from the end – Leeds were out of Europe.

Eric, meanwhile, was out of the team again for Leeds' fixture against Arsenal at the end of November. Angered by the decision, he refused to sit on the substitutes' bench, and went home. Leeds won 3–0. Elsewhere that weekend, Manchester United defeated Oldham Athletic by the same score. But, although Brian McClair scored twice and his fellow forward Mark Hughes got the other one, United were reported to be trying to sign Sheffield Wednesday striker David Hirst.

However, the real identity of United's latest purchase was revealed at a press conference held at Old Trafford on 27 November, when Ferguson announced, in his best French: '*Mon plaisir à presenter Eric Cantona*' – 'It is my pleasure to present Eric Cantona.'

Ferguson was clearly delighted with his capture, claiming: 'He's the showman to light up our stadium.' What particularly impressed the manager was the manner in which Eric entered Old Trafford. 'He just looked around and asked himself: "I'm Cantona, is this place big enough for me?"' Ferguson said. 'There is such a presence about Cantona. He is tailor-made for Old Trafford.'

The manager was also certain that United's style

of play would suit Eric better. 'He has flair, he has class, and we have now provided him with the biggest of stages upon which to perform,' Ferguson remarked, adding that he thought the Frenchman had been crucial to Leeds' Championship success. 'The most important thing is that he has tremendous ability. I hope we can add to that because at this club I think he has the potential to become a real giant.' Even Ferguson could not have known how true those words would turn out to be.

Eric himself said little. Admitting that his ten months at Leeds had been one of the best times of his career so far, he announced: 'My journey carries on and has now brought me to Manchester United. Obviously, I have been brought here to score goals, but I would also hope to bring something extra to the team.' Of the disappointed Leeds fans he had left behind, he added: 'I can understand that some people may feel that I have let them down, but I do not see it that way. I had a special relationship with those fans.'

Over at Elland Road, Wilkinson claimed everyone was satisfied by the transfer deal. 'Alex Ferguson got a player, and Eric Cantona has got a transfer which, on the face of it, offers him a greater opportunity of first-team football than that which he had here.' Not everyone in Leeds was sad to see him go either. One team-mate was quoted as saying: 'Eric should have been a tennis player or a golfer. He's an individualist, not a team player.'

His new team-mates made it plain early on that Eric would have to battle for a place in the United side. While welcoming the Frenchman's arrival, Mark Hughes warned: 'I have a job to do for United as well, and I don't intend to give up without a fight.' Brian McClair claimed: 'I'm happy to have competition, but I'll be determined to make sure I'm the one who stays in this team.' A bigger welcome came from two of United's greatest former players, George Best and Sir Bobby Charlton. 'The talent is definitely there. Cantona is one of the best players in the League, if not the most exciting in the country. The United fans will love his style of play,' Best suggested. Charlton agreed, saying: 'He could prove a real bargain.'

Eric's first match in a Manchester United shirt was on 1 December 1992, in a friendly against the Portuguese club Benfica at the Stadium of Light in Lisbon. United went down 1–0 to a goal nine minutes from the end. While Eric had a shot blocked by a defender and provided some neat passes, it was obvious that he would need some time to develop an understanding with his new colleagues.

His début in the Premiership for United came five days later in the derby clash with Manchester City at Old Trafford. He was in a position that he had become used to at Leeds – on the subs' bench – though this time it was because of a slight doubt about his fitness. Goals from Paul Ince and Hughes sealed a win for United that moved them up to fifth in the table. Coming on midway through the second half, Eric received the rather unwelcome attentions of City's tough midfielder Steve McMahon, and was clearly irritated by a couple of crunching tackles. But with one inch-perfect cross which picked out Hughes, who headed over the bar, Eric gave a glimpse of what he was capable of producing.

By the following week, he was in the first eleven for the 1–0 win over table-toppers Norwich City at Old Trafford. His influence upon United's performance was becoming apparent. Mark Hughes was among those impressed. 'For a big bloke, Eric's touch is amazing,' he commented. 'But his passes are not just for show, just for effect. They are telling balls that do a lot of damage.' On Boxing Day 1992, he registered his first goal for the club, as United came back from being 3–0 down at Sheffield Wednesday with only 22 minutes remaining to draw 3–3. When he scored again three days later, and also laid on a goal for Hughes in a 5–0 destruction of Coventry City, United moved into second place in the Premiership, only three points behind Norwich, and well placed in their attempt to become champions in the new year.

Winning the title had become something of an obsession at Old Trafford. Since their last such triumph in 1967, every Manchester United team had been weighed down by the burden of being expected to repeat that success by the club's supporters all over the world, and each season that they failed only made that burden heavier. A succession of managers tried to follow the example of United's legendary boss Sir Matt Busby.

He had built up a highly promising young team, which was christened the 'Busby Babes', only to see many of its finest members, like the gifted Duncan Edwards, tragically killed in the 1958 Munich air disaster, when the team's plane crashed on the runway as it was about to bring them home from a European tie. Busby, who only just survived the crash himself, was forced to start again. By 1967 his new line-up, including Bobby Charlton, Denis Law, Brian Kidd, Nobby Stiles and, of course, George Best, had won the title. The following season they crowned that achievement by becoming the first English club to lift the European Cup, beating Benfica 4–1 at Wembley.

Since Busby's retirement, the manager's chair had been filled by the likes of Tommy Docherty, Dave Sexton and Ron Atkinson. But although the club recovered from its lowest point – being relegated for one season in the mid-Seventies – to win the FA Cup on a number of occasions, that was not enough for United's demanding fans. They had watched as their near neighbours Liverpool enjoyed a run of seemingly endless success, winning the League Championship year after year, and then copying United's success in the European Cup – not just once, but four times in the Seventies and Eighties.

Since arriving in 1988, Alex Ferguson had led United to the FA Cup, League Cup and European Cup-Winners' Cup. But even he was under huge pressure to win the prize that had now eluded the club for 26 years. The last-gasp failure of the previous season – when Leeds had snatched the title with the help of a certain Eric Cantona – had been a terrible blow. Some United fans were beginning to wonder gloomily whether the team was doomed never to be more than runners-up.

So, even when United really began to move into top gear in January, there were many who hardly dared to hope that this time it might be different. A 4–1 victory over Tottenham Hotspur, with Eric at the heart of all that United did, had everyone who saw it marvelling at the skill on show – especially from the Frenchman. Among those spectators was George Best, who declared: 'If he keeps doing it, this club is going to win the title. That's how important he is to United. He has given this team a brain. I honestly had my doubts about him fitting in, but he has convinced me that – at just £1.1 million – he is Alex Ferguson's shrewdest signing.'

Eric was flattered by such praise from the old master. 'I'm very honoured for that comment to come from George,' he admitted, but he certainly deserved it, scoring once and having a hand in the other goals. Nor were Spurs push-overs, having won their previous three matches. The statistics also illustrated Eric's effect on United. Before his arrival, the club had managed just four goals in nine games. In the nine games since he joined, United had banged in 22 goals.

In February, Eric ran into his first controversy at United. After making his first trip back to Elland Road since leaving Leeds only three months previously, Eric, who was heckled and abused throughout the match, was found guilty of spitting at a Leeds fan. The Football Association fined him £1,000 and warned him about his future behaviour. It was another example of how Eric could let his temper get the better of him.

United were knocked out of the FA Cup fifth round in the same month by Sheffield United, 2–1. In theory, this should have left the club free to concentrate completely on winning the Premiership. In reality, United began to get the jitters which had ruined so many previous title challenges just when it appeared they were on the home straight. On 9 March, they lost 1–0 at lowly Oldham. The following week they scrambled a 1–1 draw at Old Trafford, after being a goal behind to their main rivals for the Premiership, Aston Villa. Both clubs were on 61 points after playing 33 games each. It was now a matter of whose nerve held.

Ferguson saw Eric's role in this neck-and-neck contest as vital. 'I think the rest of the team have to give Eric more responsibility and provide him with more of the ball,' he said. 'He is a marvellous player and has been fantastic for us. My belief is that Eric's got to be given more possession when he is in the penalty area – or anywhere else for that matter. He is such an attacking threat.'

Eric proved the manager's point in the last week of March, when he headed the equalizer to earn a 1–1 draw at Manchester City. But, on the same day, Villa went two points clear at the top, defeating Sheffield Wednesday 2–0. Even when Villa then lost at Norwich, United failed to take full advantage, allowing themselves to be held to a goalless draw at Old Trafford by Arsenal.

As the season drew to a close, there was still barely any daylight between United and Villa. Eric's tenth goal for the club since joining contributed to a 3–0 drubbing of Chelsea. But the following day, Villa underlined the seriousness of their bid for the title with a 3–1 victory that took them one point ahead, with three games to play for both clubs.

The crunch came on the evening of Wednesday 21 April. The pressure finally seemed to get to Villa, who collapsed 3–0 at Blackburn Rovers. United, meanwhile, met Crystal Palace at Selhurst Park, a ground which, in the not-too-distant future, would come to have such unpleasant associations for Eric. Not on this night however. In another starring performance, he set up both goals for Hughes and Ince. Since the days of Best and Charlton, this was the closest United had been to winning the title. With only two games remaining, they were four points clear.

As it turned out, United did not need to kick another ball finally to realize their 26-year-old dream. Villa threw away any lingering hopes that they had of staying in the title race by losing 1–0 at home to Oldham. With only one game left, they could no longer catch United. The following day, Monday 3 May, a carnival atmosphere welcomed United at Old Trafford, as 40,447 spectators packed into the ground to salute the new champions. To celebrate their triumph, United thumped Blackburn 3–1, with goals from Giggs, Ince and Pallister. At the final whistle, team captain Steve Bruce and long-time leader Bryan Robson lifted the brand-new Premiership trophy together, and the jubilant team paraded it around the pitch. The following week, they ended a magnificent season with a 2–1 win at Wimbledon. After enduring such nail-biting competition from Villa all season, United finished ten points clear.

At the civic dinner held in the team's honour shortly afterwards, the players arrived wearing club blazers and trousers – except Eric. He turned up in a £1,000 loose-fitting silk jacket with a T-shirt underneath. Seeing the manager, he shrugged his shoulders and said: 'On the ticket it said casual dress, I'm casual.' Ferguson resisted the joking demands of Eric's team-mates that he fine the Frenchman two weeks' wages.

It was Eric's second successive Championship medal, and his fourth including the two he had won in France while at Marseille – an extraordinary achievement. There were reports that Barcelona boss Johan Cruyff was keen to sign Eric. But Ferguson was confident that his most valuable player was going nowhere. 'I sincerely believe Eric could not get a better arena for his talents anywhere in the world,' he said.

Eric would certainly have had problems finding a more successful club. United started the 1993/94 season where they had left off, sweeping all before them with a brand of football that was always attractive and often breathtaking. At the end of August, in brilliant sunshine, Eric scored another spectacular goal at the Dell, home of Southampton, with a chip over the goalkeeper which left the crowd gasping in admiration. Southampton's keeper, Tim Flowers, said afterwards: 'From the minute the ball left his foot, I knew it was in. Not many players have the vision to do something like that. I'd say there are three players in the League who could pull that off. We've got one in Matthew Le Tissier, and United have the other two – Cantona and Giggs.' Not content with his strike, Eric also set up goals for Lee Sharpe and Denis Irwin, in a 3–1 win. United were already top of the table. A few days later, they were three points clear, after demolishing a helpless West Ham 3–0. No prizes for guessing who scored from the penalty spot and also had a hand in the first goal for Sharpe.

United also opened their European Cup campaign successfully. Their first opponents were Honved, from the Hungarian capital of Budapest, where the first leg ended 2–2. The tie was settled in a 2–1 win at Old Trafford. In the draw for the second round, United were paired with Galatasaray, the Turkish champions, and strongly fancied to beat them. But a nasty surprise was round the corner.

In the first leg at Old Trafford, the tie seemed to be going to form, when United raced into a 2–0 lead inside 13 minutes. Robson struck first and then Turkish international defender Hakan headed into his own goal under pressure from Pallister at a corner kick. The capacity crowd could hardly contain itself. Then, just as swiftly, it was silenced. The Turks pulled a goal back within three minutes. Suddenly United's defence was swamped by wave after wave of Galatasaray attacks, and were rescued only by Peter Schmeichel's exceptional goalkeeping.

But even he could do nothing about the next two goals which the Turks rattled in. United were behind at home to a team considered the underdog and beginning to panic. Nine minutes from the end, Eric chested down a lob from new signing Roy Keane, and struck a half-volley into the net, to much relief around Old Trafford. But 3–3 was hardly the result United wanted to take to Turkey for the return leg, and Alex Ferguson was scathing about the lack of teamwork. 'We get off to a flying start, put a couple of goals in the bag, then two or three of our players start turning it into a one-man show,' he fumed.

'When you are in that position, with so much at stake, it is hard to believe they can do that.'

Despite this major setback, United continued to rampage through the Premiership. A 1–0 defeat of Everton the weekend after the Galatasaray disaster put the club nine points ahead of its nearest rival after only 12 games. By the time of their 2–1 win over QPR before they travelled to Turkey, that lead had stretched to 11 points.

The visit to Istanbul will stay for ever in the memory of the players, officials and fans who made it. Galatasaray's supporters had promised United that they would be given a hostile reception, and Ferguson was in no doubt that this would be the case, as he recalled from an earlier trip he had made: 'When I was there they were chucking around golf balls and bottles.'

It was into this frightening atmosphere that United emerged on the night of 3 November to attempt to save their European ambitions. But it was not to be. Lacking ideas and invention, United were held to a goalless draw, and Galatasaray qualified for the next stage of the competition on the away-goals rule. And that was just the beginning of their troubles.

Eric's short-fused temper had almost blown in the 76th minute when, frustrated by the Turks' time-wasting tactics, he raced on to the running track around the pitch to rescue the ball after it went out of play, and ended up in an angry confrontation with the players on the Galatasaray bench. Then, when the final whistle blew, he rushed over and confronted Swiss referee Kurt Rothlisberger, complaining that no injury time had been added on. The referee showed him the red card.

At this point, Eric was escorted from the pitch, amid chaotic scenes, by a Turkish policeman and Bryan Robson, who later recalled what happened next. 'Eric was between the two of us walking slowly and saying nothing. He seemed to have cooled down totally by the time we reached the top of the tunnel steps. About 20 or 30 policemen with riot shields were gathered round the exit. I paused to let Eric go down the steps first and turned to thank the policeman for helping us.'

As Robson did so, the policeman lunged forward and struck Eric on the back of the head, sending him stumbling down the flight of concrete steps to the underground dressing-room. Robson tried to intervene and was hit by a riot shield, gashing his hand, which later required stitches, and defender Paul Parker was also attacked. In the heat of the moment, Eric then gave an interview to a French television team, in which he appeared to suggest that the referee had been bribed. The furious match official complained to UEFA, and Eric was banned for four matches in European club competitions. The general view seemed to be that he was lucky to escape a heavier punishment.

The Galatasaray tie was a nightmare for United,

and not just because it meant they were knocked out of the tournament. As the team's bus left the Istanbul stadium, louts hurled bricks at it, one of which nearly shattered the window at which Steve Bruce was sitting. Many supporters were also threatened and beaten up. Others were thrown into police cells for the night (including one 71-year-old pensioner who was dragged from his hotel bed in the middle of the night), and then thrown out of the country.

With their European Cup hopes dashed, United headed for home, and a Premiership table in which they were so far ahead that they already looked impossible to catch. Still in the League Cup, and with the FA Cup about to start, the stage was set for the Red Devils to prove their total domination of English football.

CHAPTER FOUR

United at the Double

B Y THE START OF December 1993, Manchester United were a team apart. Not only was no one else in the country playing such exciting and attacking football, but they were 14 points clear of nearest rivals Leeds. At the end of the previous month, another goal by Eric had given them a 1-0 win over Coventry City.

No wonder that Alex Ferguson was the envy of his fellow managers. He had assembled a £30 million team at Old Trafford which, despite its failure to progress in the European Cup, was looking unbeatable on these shores. It was a collection of great individual players, from numerous different countries, who combined to become an irresistible force.

Besides Eric, the foreign imports included goalkeeper Peter Schmeichel, who had played in the Denmark side which defeated Germany 2-0 in the 1992 European Championships final. Generally regarded as the world's number one keeper, the towering Schmeichel posed a formidable barrier for strikers to beat, and that was if they first got past a defence which included England internationals Steve Bruce, Gary Pallister and Paul Parker, and Irishman Denis Irwin.

It was a sign of the quality in the United line-up that veteran captain Bryan Robson, who had led the club to three FA Cup victories in 1983, 1985 and 1990, found it difficult to get a game. His successor, both at club and increasingly at national level, was Paul Ince. A tigerish tackler and tireless runner, he was nicknamed 'the Guv'nor' for the way he bossed the middle of the field. He was partnered by the talented and tough Irish midfielder Roy Keane, signed from Nottingham Forest the previous season.

But it was on the flanks that United were particularly deadly. On the left was Ryan Giggs, the young Welshman who had broken into the first team in his teens. He was already being compared to George Best because of his extraordinary ball control and dribbling skill. On the opposite wing, Ukrainian-born Andrei Kanchelskis similarly terrorized defences with his sheer speed. With Giggs and Kanchelskis coming down either wing, and Eric, partnered by the battering-ram Welsh forward Mark Hughes streaming down the middle of the pitch, bewildered opposing teams invariably did not know which way to turn.

Aston Villa had been the latest victims, just before

Christmas, as United romped to a 3–1 win over the nearest challengers to their title the previous season. By the time this game was over, Villa were far behind in the chasing pack. The victory was courtesy of two goals from Eric, who ran his marker, England international Earl Barrett, ragged, and one from Ince. Eric claimed: 'It is the best side I have ever played in. Yes, I think we are now better than we were when we won the championship last season.'

While United were too professional to take much notice of the media pundits who predicted that the title race was all over by New Year's Day, it certainly appeared unlikely that anyone was going to come near them. Everyone was already talking about United achieving what only three clubs – Tottenham Hotspur in 1961, Arsenal in 1971 and Liverpool in 1986 – had previously managed: the League and Cup Double. But, as a trip to Anfield in the first week of 1994 proved, they were not invincible.

However, Liverpool could have been forgiven for thinking the opposite in the first 24 minutes of that clash. By that stage, United were already three goals up – through Bruce, Giggs and Irwin – and turning on the sort of display which suggested they were ready to massacre their old rivals. But within a minute of United going 3–0 ahead, Nigel Clough pulled a goal back for the Merseysiders, and seven minutes from half-time, he scored again. The marvellous end-to-end action which both teams produced continued in the second half. However,

United did not convert their chances into further goals, and after 79 minutes, Liverpool defender Neil Ruddock completed his team's tremendous recovery, to make it 3–3. Afterwards, Ruddock said: 'For United to lose a three-goal lead might start them thinking and put extra pressure on them.' The clubs trailing far behind the Reds in the Premiership hoped he was right.

In the same month, United were held 2–2 in the Coca-Cola Cup quarter-final by First Division Portsmouth, despite Eric's 15th goal of the season. Ferguson revealed afterwards that he had wanted to rest Eric, but the Frenchman had insisted on playing. 'He has great character,' the manager said. 'Mind you, if I left him out I would probably never see him again!' United won the replay, and moved a step nearer their first Wembley final of the season.

Old Trafford went into mourning on 20 January that year. Sir Matt Busby, the man responsible for so much of the Manchester United legend, died, aged 84. Thousands flocked to the ground, down the recently renamed Sir Matt Busby Way, to place bouquets of flowers, scarves and messages under the clock which was a memorial to the victims of the 1958 Munich air disaster that had nearly also claimed Sir Matt's life.

The club's Premiership pennant flew at half-mast as a mark of respect. One message summed up the general sense of loss felt in the city. It read: 'You planted the seeds that have made Manchester

United the greatest team in the world. Rest in peace, Sir Matt, you have left us in safe hands.' A deeply saddened Alex Ferguson spoke for all the players when he said: 'It would be marvellous to win the Double as a lasting memorial to Sir Matt.'

A minute's silence was observed in his honour at grounds around the country the following weekend – nowhere more so, of course, than at Old Trafford, where the United players, their opponents Everton, and more than 44,000 spectators did not make a single sound for the 60 seconds. Not surprisingly perhaps, the teams, both wearing black armbands, played a somewhat subdued game, which United won with a goal from Ryan Giggs. While Ince, Keane and Kanchelskis all caught the eye at times, it was Eric whose performance again towered over everyone else's, as he hit the woodwork more than once, and was constantly in the thick of things.

Everton's then manager, Mike Walker, was full of admiration for United – and Eric – despite losing. He said: 'There is an aura about United. They are streets ahead of the rest and their players know it. There is a swaggering arrogance about them and this is not a criticism. It comes with confidence and winning lots of games. Their movement is brilliant. They interchange and you have no idea where their next move is coming from. You plug one hole and another one opens up. You fill that, another player comes at you.' Walker believed the Frenchman's contribution to United's playing style was particularly important: 'He brought it all together last season. His presence has allowed the others to play better. You can see that.'

Trouble, unfortunately, was not far away for both United and Eric. They travelled to East Anglia in the fourth round of the FA Cup to face Norwich City and defeated the Canaries 2–0, with Eric intercepting a poor pass to round the goalkeeper and put United on the road to the next round. But their outstanding performance was overshadowed by an off-the-ball incident, when Eric was captured by the television cameras aiming a kick at defender John Polston. He had already been booked in the first half for a bad challenge on another Norwich player. But, on that occasion, the referee had not seen what had happened, and Eric escaped, when most observers agreed that he should have been sent off. Among them was the BBC's commentator Jimmy Hill, who described the Frenchman's kick as 'despicable'. A row broke out as Alex Ferguson reacted by attacking Hill for his comments. It was the sort of publicity which Eric and United could do without.

After a 3–2 win at QPR in the Premiership a week later, Ferguson's thoughts had returned to matters on the pitch, as he admitted for the first time that the previously unheard of treble of Premiership, FA Cup and Coca-Cola Cup might be achievable. 'Nothing is impossible,' he said. 'We are treating it as an extra and this game has made us more relaxed about it.' Kanchelskis, Giggs and

Eric were all on top form and all on the score sheet.

Having also narrowly beaten Sheffield Wednesday 1–0 in the first leg of the Coca-Cola Cup semi-final, United continued their search for success on all fronts with a traditionally difficult trip to play Wimbledon in the FA Cup fifth round. Wimbledon, well known for knocking more stylish teams out of their stride, were utterly outplayed in a one-sided exhibition by United. Eric opened the scoring with a right-foot rocket from the edge of the penalty area, which sailed past the goalkeeper, and went close on at least one other occasion. Even Vinny Jones, who was booked for bringing Eric down, could not spoil what many present called United's best performance of the season.

United, however, almost immediately bettered it. Sheffield Wednesday were practically reduced to the status of spectators at Hillsborough in the return leg of the Coca-Cola Cup semi-final, as United went two goals ahead in the first ten minutes, and ran out eventual 4–1 winners – even though Eric was out, injured. Now in the final of one competition, and very well placed in the other two, the treble was the talk of the media and Manchester. Poor Wednesday were to be thrashed 5–0 by United in the Premiership only a fortnight later – Eric scoring twice – to leave manager Trevor Francis expressing his relief that they did not have to meet again that season.

The title race, meanwhile, was taking a fresh twist.

Slowly, but surely, Blackburn Rovers had been cutting back United's once enormous lead at the top of the table. In the past couple of seasons, manager Kenny Dalglish had taken the club into the Premiership from the First Division, backed by the fortune of local multi-millionaire Jack Walker, which allowed Blackburn to compete with anyone in the transfer market. Their most important buy was Alan Shearer, whose goal-scoring exploits had pushed his team into second place, from where they now posed a growing threat to United.

That danger increased when United stumbled at Stamford Bridge. Chelsea, who were the only team to have beaten them so far all season, completed a Premiership double over United, winning 1–0. It was United's first defeat in 34 games. Blackburn were now only four points behind, and closing. Eric was having problems off the field too. He claimed in a book that Howard Wilkinson had forced him out of Leeds, an accusation which Wilkinson swiftly denied in the press, in what became a very public argument. There was much worse to come.

United were away from home at bottom of the table Swindon Town and leading 2–1, when Eric became involved in a tussle for the ball with opposing midfield player John Moncur, who tried to slide tackle him. Eric reacted by bringing his foot down on Moncur's chest and was instantly sent off. Swindon equalized soon after to grab a draw. Critics talked about the dark side of the Frenchman and demanded that he be heavily punished. He was – fined two weeks' wages by the club and banned for three games by the FA. His last game before that suspension began was away at Arsenal.

For the second time in four days, Eric got his marching orders. He was booked in the 87th minute of a hectic match, with the score-line standing at 2–2, for a two-footed challenge upon Ian Selley. Then, in the final minute, he clashed with Arsenal skipper Tony Adams and was shown the red card. Slow-motion replays later suggested that Eric had been harshly treated for the second bookable offence. The damage, though, was done. United's ten remaining men hung on for a draw, but they had won only one of their last five games. Alex Ferguson admitted: 'The pressure is draining my players both mentally and physically.'

Eric, meanwhile, was now banned for five games. His absence from so many vital games, on top of the widespread criticism, provoked fears that he might walk out of Old Trafford. But Ferguson denied the rumours: 'There is not the slightest suggestion from Eric that he is disillusioned or ready to leave.' The manager added: 'There is a spark in him which sometimes flares up and he knows he has to behave. He can't take the law into his own hands.' Eric himself vowed that he would not turn his back on English football, or let the events of the past four days affect him: 'In France it would have been different. Here, with Manchester United, I feel

I am in the hearts of the supporters, the players and manager Alex Ferguson.'

On the following Sunday, United met Aston Villa in the Coca-Cola Cup final, and the treble that they were chasing disintegrated. Villa deservedly won 3–1, with the Reds a pale shadow of their normal selves. To complete a thoroughly miserable day, Kanchelskis was sent off in the final minute for deliberately handling the ball on the goal-line. From the resulting penalty, Villa hit the third and final goal. Except for one cross which Giggs headed over the bar after only five minutes, Eric failed to play the sort of game which might have put his problems behind him.

His last game before his long suspension saw United beat Liverpool 1–0 at Old Trafford. They were six points clear of Blackburn, with eight games left to play, when the two teams clashed at Ewood Park. Shearer struck twice to sink United, and inflict the most intense pressure yet on their hopes of the Double. With the season reaching its climax, they scrambled a 3–2 win over struggling Oldham Athletic to maintain their slender three-point lead in the Premiership, and then prepared to face the same team in the FA Cup semi-final.

That year, both semi-finals were held at Wembley. In the first, Chelsea defeated Luton Town 2–0 to book a return trip to the stadium. The next day, United looked tense and uninspired against an Oldham team striving for their first-ever Cup final appearance, and at the end of 90 minutes, the sides were deadlocked. In extra time Schmeichel, of all people, dropped a cross, and Neil Pointon stabbed the ball into the back of the net.

As Eric watched helpless from the bench on the touch-line, the clock ticked away on the electronic scoreboards above the goal-mouths. Oldham clung on, and a season which had started so brightly suddenly seemed to be crashing around United's heads. Denied a treble by Aston Villa on the same pitch, and with Blackburn breathing down their necks in the Premiership, it seemed their hopes of winning the FA Cup were also fading fast.

A mere 40 seconds remained on the clock, when a despairing pass dropped invitingly in front of Mark Hughes as he faced the Oldham goal. Without stopping to let the ball hit the ground, the Welsh international smashed home a volley which almost burst the back of the net. United were out of jail with almost the final kick of the game. As the whistle blew seconds later, it was United who celebrated while Oldham's players sank to the turf in despair. The Double was still possible.

Oldham never really recovered from the shock of Hughes's last-gasp equalizer, and crashed 4–1 to United in the replay three days later. Kanchelskis, who, like Eric, had been badly missed in the first game, came back from injury to score, along with Irwin, Robson and Giggs. United would be going to Wembley for their second final of the season –

this time, hopefully, with a rather different outcome.

There was one bright spot for Eric during his suspension. He was voted Player of the Year by his fellow professionals, pipping Peter Beardsley of Newcastle United, who was second, and Alan Shearer in third place. United showed that they were still feeling his absence by losing 1–0 at Wimbledon. Fortunately for them, Blackburn slipped up too, defeated by Southampton 3–1. Even so, the two of them were now dead level at the top of the Premiership on 79 points, with only superior goal difference keeping United in first spot.

Eric announced his return in the most certain terms. With the strains of the French national anthem, the 'Marseillaise', ringing in his ears from the Old Trafford faithful, he repaid their welcome by scoring twice in a five-minute period before half-time against neighbours Manchester City. He blotted his copybook slightly by bringing down City's German striker Uwe Rosler. But the roar from the Stretford End left no one in any doubt: Eric was back.

What was even better from the Old Trafford point of view was that Blackburn could manage only a draw on the same weekend, putting United two points clear and with the added bonus of a game in hand. Confidence was clearly returning to the team at the same time as Blackburn were beginning to feel the pressure and make errors. At the beginning of May, with the FA Cup final a fortnight away,

United moved to within one point of the title. They won 2–1 at Ipswich Town – who were fighting to stay in the Premiership – after Ipswich had taken the lead. Inevitably, it was Eric who headed the equalizer, from a Kanchelskis cross, and Giggs wrapped it up two minutes after half-time.

A day later, United were champions for the second successive season. Blackburn slumped 2–1 at Coventry City. It was a remarkable triumph for the club, which had waited 26 years to win the title, and had now claimed two in a row. Although it had been another long slog, Alex Ferguson said the pressure had not been quite as great as previously. 'Yes, it was harder the first time,' he said. 'Last year it felt like the whole weight of history was against us.'

For Eric, it was yet another addition to his incredible record: three seasons in England, three Championship medals. Ferguson could not praise him enough: 'Eric is quite unbelievable. The man is without doubt a truly great player. After all his achievements with us, he now deserves to be ranked alongside the all-time greats who have played for United.' The question on everyone's lips was: could United complete the Double?

Their opponents on Saturday 14 May were Chelsea, the team that had already beaten them twice in the Premiership that season. In the first half, it looked as if the same might happen again. The so-called underdogs were far more effective than

United, and when Gavin Peacock rattled the crossbar with Schmeichel beaten, you could hear the sigh of relief from the red and white end of Wembley. United were fortunate to go in at half-time with the scoreline still 0–0.

The turning-point came early in the second half. Chelsea defender Eddie Newton fouled Denis Irwin, and the referee pointed to the penalty spot, without hesitating. Neither did Eric Cantona. Scooping up the ball, he placed it firmly on the spot. As he did so, Chelsea's Dennis Wise went over to speak to him. It was revealed later that Wise had bet Eric £100 that he would miss the penalty. It was a trick he had tried successfully before. But he had not tried it before with this particular penalty-taker. The calmest man in the entire stadium stepped up and sidefooted the ball into the bottom right-hand corner of the net as Chelsea's Russian goalkeeper, Dimitri Kharine, went the wrong way.

Shortly afterwards, United won a second penalty, after the referee judged that Kanchelskis had been brought down, which looked rather unfair on Chelsea. Eric repeated his earlier feat, and the game was over as a contest, with United putting another two goals past a by now demoralized Chelsea. Asked if he had been nervous as he prepared to take the penalties, Eric said: 'If you don't want to take penalties in a match like this, then you should pack up playing football. It did not enter my head that I would not score.' Dennis Wise, meanwhile, was as good as his word and paid up the £100. 'I told him not to be so stupid because Eric Cantona doesn't miss penalties in a Cup final. I didn't think he'd pay but he did – he's good like that, a great man,' Eric said.

Goalkeeper Schmeichel, who watched the penalty drama from the other end of the pitch, was also certain that Eric would score. The Frenchman's regular room-mate on United's travels claimed: 'When I saw Eric put the ball on the spot, I knew the Double was safe. I have been in that position with him at least 2,500 times in training and he doesn't miss often.' For Eric, the feeling of delight at winning the Double could not be compared: 'When I was a boy I wanted to play football like this. To play for a club like this. I did not know it would happen. But it has and I know this is only the start for Manchester United. It is the best team I have played in and I believe the target for Manchester United should be to win everything.'

Alex Ferguson was also looking to the future, saying: 'The most important thing now is tomorrow. My dearest wish is to win the European Cup next season, to do ourselves proud in that competition. This team is capable of doing a European Cup and Premiership Double.' Its astonishing record over the Double-winning 1993/94 season certainly seemed to back Ferguson's claim. United had scored 126 goals in all competitions, and lost only six out of 64 games. More importantly, they had lived up to their pledge to win the Double in memory of Sir Matt Busby. As he watched his players parading the Cup round Wembley on their lap of honour, Ferguson said: 'How Sir Matt would have loved to have been here. Sir Matt would have been proud.'

Eric continued to grab the headlines at the end of the season. Inter Milan were reported to be interested in taking him to Italy in a swap with Dennis Bergkamp, their Dutch striker, who would eventually, of course, join Arsenal. Then, at the World Cup in the United States that summer, Eric was again the centre of attention for the wrong reasons.

He had gone to the tournament as a commentator for French television, as France, like England, had failed to qualify for the finals. He was due to cover the semi-final between Brazil and Sweden when he was refused entry to the stadium by security guards, who later claimed that Eric did not have the correct pass. A scuffle broke out and finished with the Frenchman being arrested and led away in handcuffs, though he was soon released without being charged.

In a pre-season competition in Scotland, Eric ran into yet more trouble. He was sent off for an over the top tackle on a Glasgow Rangers defender at Ibrox Park, after first being booked for walking away when the referee was talking to him. Ferguson admitted: 'He simply can't control his temper in these situations. We just have to work on his faults.' But captain Steve Bruce said what a lot of people were thinking when he commented: 'Eric wears his heart on his sleeve and what you see is what you get. I don't think we will ever change that.'

Eric would soon prove him right – at great cost to himself and to Manchester United.

Early days

*Eric riding on his favourite motorbike,
a Harley Davidson*

Relaxing and painting

Signing for Manchester United

The King of Old Trafford

Eric is always perfecting his ball skills

Celebrating a goal against Liverpool with Roy Keane –
October 1 1995

A vital equalizer against Sheffield Wednesday –
December 9 1995

Player of the Year 1996

Captain of the FA Cup Winning Team –
May 11 1996

Eric wins his third Premiership title with
Manchester United – May 1996

CHAPTER FIVE

25 January 1995

Looking back, it always seemed likely that Eric was going to explode that night. Right from the kick-off of the Premiership clash with Crystal Palace at the south London club's Selhurst Park ground, he repeatedly complained to the referee about some of the tackles he was receiving. His mood appeared to be as black as the away strip in which United were playing.

In the 48th minute, Palace defender Richard Shaw caught Eric from behind, a clumsy challenge which went unpunished, as referee Alan Wilkie failed to notice a linesman flagging for the incident. Moments later, Eric needlessly kicked out at Shaw in a fit of rage, as the pair went for a high clearance from Peter Schmeichel. This was instantly spotted by the match officials, and referee Wilkie ran over to Eric in front of the main stand to show him the red card. It was his fifth sending off in 16 months.

The scowling Frenchman turned on his heel and stalked off towards the players' tunnel. As he did so, he ran a gauntlet of abuse from the seething main stand. The most visible of his tormentors was a sandy-haired young man in a leather jacket and light-grey trousers. He had raced down a set of steps to the family enclosure at the front of the stand as soon as Eric received his marching orders and was now swearing venomously, as well as making obscene gestures at the departing player.

And, at that precise moment – 8.57 p.m. on 25 January 1995 – something in Eric Cantona snapped.

Eric had begun that fateful 1994/95 season under a cloud. Already banned from four European Cup ties following the disastrous night against Galatasaray in Turkey, he was then hit with a further three-match suspension for his sending off in the pre-season friendly against Rangers. His former Marseille and France team-mate Basile Boli, who had just joined the Scottish champions, warned: 'Eric hasn't changed and there's no way he can. He's impulsive. He's like a bull, he sees red. He comes from Marseille and has Latin blood in him. There's no way you can stop him.' In an interview at around the same time, Eric appeared to agree: 'Things don't seem to be going all that well with referees, but it's in my character to play the way I do. It's in my blood, it's my nature. It's that very nature that makes me react the way I do.' Not all referees were unsympathetic, however. One former leading ref, Keith Hackett, claimed: 'People are out to get him sent off. People have always been aware of his temper, but now he's showing it and some defenders are using it to their advantage.'

Others, however, were using Eric's high profile to their advantage. Sportswear firm Nike featured him in an award-winning advertisement, in front of a St George's cross flag, which played upon England's World Cup victory 28 years before, with the message: ''66 was a great year for English football, Eric was born.' Even here though, he could not totally escape controversy. Another of his Nike commercials was banned from television for including a swear word.

His last game before the three-match Premiership ban was yet another trip to Wembley, where he became the first man to play in three successive FA Charity Shield victories. United beat the previous season's Premiership runners-up, Blackburn Rovers, 2−0, with Eric scoring the opener from the penalty spot and then setting up the second for Paul Ince. Nor did United appear to suffer particularly from his enforced absence once the season proper began.

A 2−0 defeat of Queen's Park Rangers on the first Saturday was followed by a midweek 1−1 draw at Nottingham Forest, and then a 1−0 victory at Tottenham Hotspur. Even so, observers commented that without their French star, United seemed to lack a certain inspiration and flair. On his return against Wimbledon at Old Trafford, at the end of

August, it quickly became apparent exactly what United had been missing.

Even before he put the team ahead in the 40th minute, with a header from a cross supplied by Giggs, Eric's vision and precise passing had almost provided United with three goals. McClair and Giggs did actually find the back of the net later on, to complete a clear-cut victory, and it seemed as though normal service was being resumed: Manchester United were out to win everything again. To the concern of their Premiership rivals, it looked like they might just do exactly that.

As Alex Ferguson had made plain in the wake of the Double triumph, what United really wanted to win, however, was the European Cup. In a change to the tournament's usual format, the qualifying teams had this year been put into four groups of four, with the top two from each eventually going on to contest the quarter-finals on the usual knock-out basis. United had been drawn with IFK Gothenburg of Sweden, the Spanish champions Barcelona, and, worst of all, Galatasaray, which meant they would have to go back to the scene of the previous season's horror story in Turkey.

Their first tie, without Eric of course, was at home to Gothenburg, and the preparation for the big game was hardly ideal: a 1–0 defeat at Leeds United, who had not beaten United before for 13 years. It also put United back to fifth in the table. As it turned out, they still managed to defeat the Swedes in a thrilling 4–2 battle, Giggs scoring twice. But they looked shaky in doing so, and had to fight back from falling behind early on before settling it.

In the Premiership, meanwhile, the always eagerly awaited clash with Liverpool finished in a 2–0 win at Old Trafford. But the match also provided evidence of how opponents were determined to wind Eric up and niggle him at every opportunity. Liverpool defender Neil Ruddock persistently made a point of turning down Eric's collar whenever they were close, and he was also accused of catching the Frenchman with his elbow in an incident which the referee did not notice. Later, he certainly did see Eric's foul on Ruddock and out came the yellow card.

At the end of September 1994 came the dreaded return visit to Istanbul. As the team walked out, they were greeted by a banner draped over a balcony in the Turkish stadium which read: 'Welcome to Judgement Day'. If the message was ominous, the final result was not. Despite missing Eric, United played a tight defensive game which earned them a 0–0 draw, a performance that captain Steve Bruce afterwards described as 'boring but magic'. The outcome of the other game in the group on the same night gave even greater cause for hope. Barcelona surprisingly lost at Gothenburg, meaning that United were on top.

Old Trafford prepared for the arrival of the feared and respected Spanish champions. Managed by

Dutch legend Johan Cruyff – a childhood hero of Eric – Barcelona boasted an incredible array of talent from around the world. Romario, the Brazilian ace whose goals had been instrumental in his country's World Cup triumph that summer in the United States, was up front alongside the equally deadly hitman Hristo Stoichkov from Bulgaria. In midfield, there was Gheorghe Hagi of Romania, another star of USA '94. In defence was Dutchman Ronald Koeman, best known in Britain for the goal which killed England's hopes of qualifying for the World Cup, and an awesome free-kick taker.

Without Eric, United's task looked even tougher. Cruyff's assistant, Bruins Slott, who travelled over to spy on them during a 1–0 win over West Ham, agreed. 'Cantona gives the United team a feeling,' he commented. 'He dictates so much with his short passes. He can slow them down and give other attacking players more possibilities.' On the night itself, the Frenchman's absence did not at first appear to matter. Mark Hughes, playing against his old club, put United one up after 18 minutes. But Romario was not to be denied, equalizing before half-time. When Bakero gave Barcelona the lead, United's 38-year-old record of never having lost at home in a European competition was in terrible danger.

It was Lee Sharpe who saved both the record and United's hopes of progressing further in the European Cup. Only ten minutes from the end, Roy

Keane fired a low cross into the Barcelona penalty area, which Sharpe directed past the goalkeeper with a brilliant back-heel flick. United clung on to the top of European Champions Group A by goal difference. Two weeks later the two teams met again at the Nou Camp Stadium in Barcelona.

With the obvious exception of the Munich air disaster, it was probably the worst night in United's history of playing in Europe. Struggling to comply with the rules limiting the number of foreign-born players in a European tie, the team was forced to drop Schmeichel, while Eric sat out the last match of his most recent ban in the stand, a black baseball cap covering half of his face as the catastrophe was played out on the pitch below him.

Barcelona ran amok, winning 4–0, with Stoichkov scoring twice and Romario and Ferrer claiming the others. A despairing Ferguson exclaimed afterwards: 'We were well and truly slaughtered. It was a bad, bad performance – a quite humiliating experience to lose by that score.' Gothenburg's win at Galatasaray lessened even further United's chance of continuing beyond the group stage.

United's rapidly approaching visit to the Ullevi Stadium in Gothenburg now took on greater importance. Their build-up to the tie could not have been better. Manchester City were thrashed 5–0 with the help of a stunning hat trick from Andrei Kanchelskis. Eric also scored and, as usual, was involved in nearly all the other goals. Then, against Crystal Palace, they were equally dominant. Irwin, Kanchelskis and Cantona were the names on the score sheet, as United recorded their eighth win in a row, and their 11th Premiership match at Old Trafford without conceding a goal – a new record. Most importantly, however, they went to the top of the table for the first time that season.

Palace boss Alan Smith shook his head in admiration as he tried to describe Eric's impact. 'All I know is that, while we have seen £5 million players in this country, Cantona is beyond price because he is unique,' he said. 'He is in a class of his own in British football. I can't think of anyone even vaguely like him.' Smith was sure that Eric's return to action in the European Cup would make a vital difference in Gothenburg.

Unfortunately, he was wrong. United were sunk 3–1, and Ince was sent off to complete a miserable night. Eric, while providing the pass for Hughes's solitary goal, could not make that difference. To survive now, United had to beat Galatasaray at Old Trafford, and hope Gothenburg won in Barcelona on the same night. Ferguson had few illusions: 'I think we are out. I don't hold out any hope now – it's as simple as that.' Just when the club's fans were starting to think it couldn't get worse, Blackburn knocked them off the top of the Premiership.

For the match against Galatasaray, Ferguson gambled – throwing in youngsters like Gary Neville, David Beckham and Simon Davies – and it paid off: the Turks were given a 4–0 hammering. But, as the manager had suspected after the defeat in Sweden, it was too late. Barcelona scraped through on goal difference, after being held 1–1 by Gothenburg, who qualified with them. It was another cruel blow to United's – and Eric's – passionate European Cup ambitions.

At least the Premiership still seemed well within reach, as the club put together a string of seven wins in the nine games following the awful night in Barcelona. The beginning of 1995 also saw United open their latest FA Cup campaign by beating Sheffield United 2–0 in the third round. Eric sealed the success eight minutes from the end with one of his most eye-catching goals yet. Taking a pass from Giggs, he advanced to within 18 metres of the Sheffield goal-mouth, and then chipped the ball over shocked goalkeeper Alan Kelly's head, sending it spinning and curling into the roof of the net.

Eric also had a new partner up front. What looked like a long-term injury to Mark Hughes had forced Ferguson into the transfer market. In a record-breaking deal which also included winger Keith Gillespie going in the opposite direction, he bought Newcastle United's top scorer, Andy Cole, for a fee of £7 million. It was a remarkable signing, as Cole was worshipped by the Newcastle fans, who were just as upset as Leeds followers had been when Eric left them for United.

Cole made his début in the top of the table battle

with Blackburn at Old Trafford, and all eyes were upon him. But the new boy failed to score and, typically, it was Eric who stole the limelight – and the three points for United – with the headed winner. Although Blackburn still led the Premiership, United hád closed to within two points of them. The fans rubbed their hands at the prospect of seeing what looked like a deadly Cantona–Cole partnership develop. In fact, it was to be eight months before they were to see the two players in action again. For three days later, United travelled to Selhurst Park.

What should have been a straightforward fixture, even though it offered United the opportunity to go top of the Premiership, turned into one of the most notorious nights in English football history. The two-footed flying kick which Eric launched carried him over the advertising hoardings at the side of the ground, and struck the spectator in the chest, causing him to stumble backwards. The 18,000 capacity crowd at Selhurst Park was in uproar. Then, as millions of television viewers watched, Eric struggled to his feet and threw several punches at the same man. Suddenly, everybody seemed to be running towards the scene. An angry Paul Ince became caught up in the confrontation.

Finally, as police officers, match stewards and fellow players all sought frantically to break up the struggle, Eric was led away by United's kitman, Norman Davis, who had come racing off the bench, and the tall figure of Schmeichel. Before they disappeared down the tunnel, a cup of tea was flung over the group by irate Palace fans. Although it hardly seemed to matter any more, the game continued and finished in a 1–1 draw.

Ferguson, sitting in the dug-out, did not see the start of the incident, and it was only when he arrived home that night that he realized the full extent of the disaster. 'My son Jason asked if I wanted to watch the video of it,' he would remember later. 'I said, "I'll watch it tomorrow," but when I went to bed I couldn't sleep. At 5 a.m. I got up and watched it. It was terrible. I couldn't believe it. How could Eric have done it?'

Reaction elsewhere to the incident was similarly horrified. Former England striker Gary Lineker, who was covering the match for television, declared: 'It is one of the most amazing things I have ever seen. It doesn't matter how you are provoked by the crowd, or how much they abuse you, you have got to rise above it.' Another former player turned television commentator, Alan Hansen, claimed that the best thing Eric could do was to leave United voluntarily and not force them to get rid of him. 'He has no alternative but to pack his bags and find another home,' he said.

A Football Association spokesman said what everyone already knew, that charges of breaking the laws of the game would swiftly follow what the FA's Chief Executive, Graham Kelly, called 'a stain on our game'. The police also confirmed that the matter was under official investigation and that criminal charges could be brought, following complaints made against both Eric and Paul Ince. The French media accused Eric of bringing shame upon his country: 'He was giving a good image in England and he has destroyed everything in two minutes.' Even the local newspaper, the Manchester *Evening News*, had to admit in its headline the next morning: 'Ooh-Aah – He's Gone Too Far'.

Speculation mounted that Eric would join Barcelona, where Cruyff was known to be an admirer of the Frenchman's skills. One place he would not be playing was his national team, it soon became clear. Claude Simonet, President of the French Football Federation, said: 'I'm afraid it's all over for Cantona with the French team,' and stripped him of the captaincy. The first action taken against Eric, however, was by United. The club suspended him for the rest of the season and fined him two weeks' wages, estimated at £20,000, which was the maximum allowed under his contract.

It meant that Eric would miss at least 17 matches in the crucial run-up to the end of the season, with both the Premiership and FA Cup still to be won. It was the longest ban in English football since a group of players had been punished for a match-fixing scandal in 1964. United Chairman Martin Edwards claimed: 'We felt we had a duty to the game and our own reputation to think of, and that is reflected in the length of the ban.' He added that Eric had accepted the punishment.

Alex Ferguson revealed some time later that he had felt certain Eric would have to leave Old Trafford: 'I was afraid it would be impossible for Eric to play in our game after what happened. He would be under terrible pressure from the media, and the provocation at away grounds would be even worse. I felt sympathy for Eric's wife, who was pregnant and would be going through agony over the matter. I was certain Eric was haunted by it all – but I really felt we had to let him go.' After an emergency board meeting, however, it was decided that the ban and fine imposed were sufficient punishment.

The morning after the incident, staff and customers at Old Trafford's Manchester United Megastore were astonished to see Eric come through the door, looking for a replica shirt for his son, Raphael. 'It was just the normal Eric,' a member of staff recalled. 'He was as cool as a cucumber, you would have thought nothing had happened. He walked around as if he didn't have a care in the world.' At United's 5–2 victory over Wrexham in the FA Cup fourth round the following weekend, fans painted their faces red and white with the message, 'We love you, Cantona', while posters all around the ground pleaded, 'Don't go, Eric'.

Within a day of the Selhurst Park incident, it was revealed that the man Eric had attacked, 20-year-old Matthew Simmons, had a conviction for violent crime after striking a petrol pump attendant with a spanner during a raid, two years earlier. His claim that he had only said to the player, 'Off you go, Cantona, it's an early bath for you,' was greeted with ridicule. Crystal Palace announced that Simmons was banned from attending any home matches for the rest of the season.

Former top striker turned television personality Jimmy Greaves said that, while Eric's actions could not be excused, paying to watch a football match did not give anyone the right to insult players. 'A measly ten quid does not give you permission to abuse, taunt, spit, lob coins, make rude gestures, throw missiles and generally behave in a way that would get you locked up if you repeated that behaviour in the High Street,' he claimed in the *Sun* newspaper.

Others pointed out that Eric was not the first to seek revenge in the way he had. Football followers with long memories recalled that, in 1937, the famed Everton and England striker Dixie Dean had hit a spectator who had abused him as he left the field in an FA Cup tie against Tottenham. On that occasion, the police had congratulated him on his response! More recently, the former Nottingham Forest manager Brian Clough had struck spectators who ran on to the pitch in celebration during a game in 1989. He was given a £5,000 fine and a warning.

Eric was certainly not going to escape so lightly.

On 21 February, he was charged with common assault and ordered to appear before magistrates the following month. To United's disappointment, the FA also decided that the ban imposed on the player until the end of the season did not go far enough. Its three-man disciplinary commission banned him from playing football at home and abroad until 30 September, which meant he would miss the beginning of the following season too. He was also fined £10,000. This time, unlike the previous occasion in France, Eric resisted the temptation to call the commission's members anything, maintaining a total silence. Maurice Watkins, a solicitor and United director, told the FA bosses: 'Eric has never sought to justify his action or minimize its seriousness. He deeply regrets what he has done.' He had, however, been in trouble again in the mean time.

Seeking to avoid the overwhelming attention, Eric had gone on holiday with Isabelle and Raphael to the Caribbean island of Guadeloupe. But he had not succeeded entirely in shaking off the chasing media. Independent Television News (ITN) reporter Terry Lloyd followed him, and began filming the player while he was on a public beach. An infuriated Eric grabbed hold of the journalist and kicked him in the ribs. Lloyd – brother of actor Kevin Lloyd, who plays Detective Constable 'Tosh' Lines in *The Bill* – complained: 'I'm a United fan. I had thought very highly of him until I got his boot in my ribs.'

The local police took no action, confiscating the ITN camera crew's tapes instead. FA Chairman, Sir Bert Millichip, refused to criticize Eric, saying: 'I had great sympathy for him that people were chasing him all over the world. They have followed him around to take pictures of him,' adding that all the Frenchman was seeking was 'a bit of peace'. Ferguson also fiercely defended his player. 'To film without permission a man's six-month pregnant wife in her swimsuit sitting on a beach is deplorable,' he claimed. 'Any husband worth his salt would react, and the ITN interviewer has got off lightly in my view.'

Meanwhile, another footballer in trouble for a violent incident was being sent to jail. Chelsea captain and England international Dennis Wise was convicted of assaulting a taxi driver and kicking his cab, and given a three-month sentence. He was released on bail, pending an appeal, but his punishment begged the question: what would happen to Eric and Paul Ince, both due to face assault charges in court the following week?

The two players arrived at Croydon Magistrates Court on 23 March, amid massive public interest. More than 100 photographers, journalists and members of television crews thronged the building. Ince was dealt with in moments, as he pleased not guilty and had his case adjourned. Eric pleaded guilty and listened as his defending solicitor claimed that he had acted only after being heavily provoked by Simmons, who, he said had been abusive, not just about the player, but also his mother.

After spending 40 minutes deciding upon their sentence, the magistrates returned to court. Their chairman, Jean Pearch, told the Frenchman: 'You are a high-profile public figure with undoubted gifts and, as such, you are looked up to by many young people. For this reason the only sentence that is appropriate for this offence is two weeks' imprisonment.' Gasps of surprise could be heard in the public gallery, as Eric, showing no emotion, was led down the stairs from the dock to the cells below.

He was later freed on bail until the following week and his legal team said he would appeal against the sentence. But many people were stunned at the prospect of Eric being put behind bars. Lord Denning, a former leading judge, claimed that he had only been jailed because he was famous: 'It is entirely the wrong reason for sending him to prison. Punishment should not depend on whether the person is well known or not.' Sir Bobby Charlton added: 'Eric has been punished enough.'

As Eric waited for his appeal to be heard, Inter Milan once more tried to lure him to Italy, offering United a reported £5 million. The club insisted that Eric was staying, and its hopes were boosted when his two-week jail sentence was quashed, and he was ordered instead to perform 120 hours of community service with young footballers. Using the club's training ground, the Cliff, in nearby Salford, Eric worked with a total of 732 children, aged between nine and 13, over 60 coaching sessions in April and May.

Among his first pupils were the youngsters of Ellesmere Park Junior FC, who were given the following advice by someone who knew from experience what he was talking about: 'If you're going to get a yellow card, walk away and don't get into any trouble with the referee.' Simon Croft, aged 13, said: 'He was fantastic. He has always been my hero and it was great to be taught by him. He clapped my first goal. Just imagine – Eric clapping me. It's a day I won't forget.' Greater Manchester probation service, which supervised the player's sentence, said he had carried out the work in full, and that it had been of great benefit to a lot of youngsters.

Susan Wildman, a spokeswoman for the probation service, believes that the children made the disgraced star realize that he was still held in great affection. She commented: 'They were typical Salford kids. They weren't overawed at all and kept asking him, "Are you staying at United?" I'm sure it had an effect. The important thing, though, was that the children understood that he was being punished for an offence. He had to face different children every session, so he didn't have a chance to build relationships. It was repetitive, hard work that was demanding and stressful and I'm sure the novelty soon began to pall. Like everyone else serving these sentences, there comes a time around the middle and three-quarters point where it becomes very difficult. It was, however, a model sentence in many ways. Eric Cantona was punished, but Salford, which is a deprived area, benefited hugely.'

If Eric remained in any doubt about where his future lay, United made up his mind, by offering him a new and improved three-year deal to stay. Touched by the club's faith in him and the way in which it had supported him through the darkest days, the player announced he would not be leaving. Ferguson was delighted. 'The incredible way he has coped has shown me that there is hope, that he will be able to come to terms with the problems that lie ahead,' he said. Asked about the pressure he was sure to face when he returned to the game, Eric declared: 'How will I handle it? Easily. It is not a problem for me.'

Tragically, the consequences of the night of 25 January continued to be felt. Having progressed to the FA Cup semi-final, United were drawn – almost unbelievably – against Crystal Palace. They met at Villa Park in Birmingham, but before the game two coachloads of rival fans clashed in a pitched fight which left one man dead and others injured. The senseless killing, in spite of the best efforts of the two clubs to appeal for calm, cast a long shadow over the actual game, which ended 2–2. United won the replay, 2–0.

In the Premiership, United had made up ground on long-time leaders Blackburn Rovers. On the final

Sunday of the season, United needed to win at West Ham and hope that their rivals would lose to retain the title. Blackburn were indeed defeated by a last-second goal from Liverpool at Anfield. But, at Upton Park, United went behind in the first half and McClair's equalizer after 52 minutes was not enough. Blackburn were champions by one point – for the first time since 1914.

The other half of the previous year's Double that United were defending was also lost, when Everton clinched the FA Cup thanks to striker Paul Ride-out's 30th-minute Wembley winner. For the first time in five seasons, United were left without a trophy. Then, it looked as if they were about to be deprived of Eric as well, for the Frenchman suddenly demanded a transfer.

The reason behind his decision was an inquiry by the FA into a training game in which Eric took part against a team from Rochdale in July. The investigation was to see if he had broken the terms of his playing ban. But for the player it was the final straw. Although the FA quickly announced that it did not intend to pursue the matter, Eric flew to France. A concerned Ferguson soon followed him to try and persuade him to come back.

Over a meal in Paris, Eric poured his heart out to the manager, and it soon became clear that the FA inquiry was not the only reason for his unhappiness. His wife, who had by this stage given birth to a daughter, Josephine, had gone back to Marseilles on holiday with the baby and Raphael. The family had moved out of their home and were in the process of looking for somewhere new to live, so Eric had to stay in a Manchester hotel room. Alone, without even the company of his team-mates, who were away on tour, Eric had grown increasingly troubled. 'Things have preyed on his mind, and got to Eric,' Ferguson explained. However, he added that their heat-to-heart conversation had cleared the air. 'I know his future is secure with us,' Ferguson said. 'He's going to play for us when his ban ends in October. I'm certain of that. I haven't had much sleep lately, but I'm happy the job is done.' United's army of fans hoped that their manager was right, and began counting the days to their hero's return.

CHAPTER SIX

The Return of the Magnificent Seven

NO MATTER WHERE YOU looked, there were French flags. Outside the ground, his face and name were emblazoned across 19 different T-shirt designs. Fans filing into the turnstiles were confronted by a poster, paid for and designed by two of their fellow supporters, which read: 'Welcome back, Eric, from everyone who loves football.'

Once inside, they could hear seven different chants – most praising, some from the visiting fans not so complimentary – which were all about one person. That same person had attracted 108 television crews from around the world to Old Trafford and had had his face featured on the covers of more than 20 magazines in the previous month alone.

Half an hour before the start, he ran out with his team-mates for a pre-match warm-up, to an enormous roar, as the public-address system boomed out the theme tune from the film *The Magnificent Seven*. So, on Saturday 1 October 1995, as Manchester United kicked off their Premiership meeting with

Liverpool, Eric Cantona reclaimed the shirt number which he had not worn for 248 days, 18 hours and 22 minutes.

The long wait was over, and for United and their fans it could not have come quickly enough. Before his ban, Eric had been scoring a goal in every two matches on average. In his 95 appearances for the club, they had lost on only eight occasions. His close friend Peter Schmeichel admitted: 'I can't wait for his comeback. I am sure you will see a different and better Eric when he returns. He was good enough last time, but I believe he is going to be even better this time. Take a few minutes out of your life and come down to see him in training. You just wouldn't believe what he's capable of doing these days.' Schmeichel added: 'When he's back in the team, Eric will add to the confidence of the young players as well. He just never loses possession and they can learn so much from him.'

It was a rather different United team to which Eric was returning. Over the summer, big names like Paul Ince, Mark Hughes and Andrei Kanchelskis had departed. Worse, from the United fans' point of view, no replacements had been signed. Instead, Ferguson was putting his faith in a new generation of youngsters who had worked their way through the ranks from the club's youth team. They included the very promising Neville brothers, Gary and Philip, in defence, developing talents like Nicky Butt and David Beckham in midfield and, up front, the high-scoring Paul Scholes, who had been filling Eric's position during the Frenchman's absence with a confidence which suggested someone much older.

The supporters' nagging worry that the team was too inexperienced appeared to be confirmed on the opening day of the 1995/96 season, when United went three goals behind in only 37 minutes at Aston Villa. A consolation goal six minutes from the end succeeded only in making the final score-line look not quite so one-sided. There were even people asking whether or not Ferguson would be around as manager much longer.

After that, in the Premiership at least, United had found their feet. Scholes, in particular, was hitting the back of the net regularly, which was more than could be said for Andy Cole. United's most expensive player had, of course, been denied his usual striking partner as soon as he had arrived, because of Eric's ban. But that did not fully explain his failure in front of goal, and the supporters were starting to get restless. They looked at his record at his previous club, Newcastle – 68 goals in 84 appearances – and demanded he do the same at Old Trafford.

Even so, United were keeping up with Newcastle, who, as the early pace-setters under manager Kevin Keegan, had made a flying start. In other competitions, however, it was all going badly wrong, especially the Coca-Cola Cup, where the club suffered a huge shock. York City were a struggling outfit who were one off the bottom of the Second Division. They had won only one match so far that season, and even then it had been gained with the help of an own goal.

But, a week and a half before Eric's return, York shamed United in one of the biggest upsets that the competition had seen, winning 3–0 at Old Trafford. Ferguson fumed about the lack of effort from his young players against the smaller club. Six days later, they were making their exit from the UEFA Cup too. The opponents this time were the Russian side Rotor Volgograd.

In the first leg away from home, United had performed creditably in a goal-less draw. They hardly knew what had hit them in the second leg. Old Trafford was plunged into a deathly silence as United were caught napping twice in the first 24 minutes. They were still 2–0 down at half-time. Scholes pulled one back early in the second half, and United threw everything at Volgograd's buckling defence in an effort to overcome the deficit. Butt had two chances cleared off the line, Pallister was denied three times by similar last-ditch clearances, and both Bruce and Cole struck the woodwork. In the final minute, Schmeichel raced upfield into the Russians' penalty area as Giggs took a corner and, incredibly, he headed the equalizer. But it was not enough. United went out on the away-goals rule.

After the game, the last before Eric's return, Ferguson proclaimed: 'Eric Cantona can win us the title again. This season, too.' It was a sign of the belief that the manager had always shown in his favourite player. Now it was up to Eric to live up to that expectation. As the Liverpool game approached, his old rival Neil Ruddock warned: 'Now that he is back he cannot expect to be treated any differently from anyone else. He is not a special case in my book.' Steve Bruce pleaded for his team-mate to be given a chance. 'He is a special talent,' the captain said. 'It will be a shame if he's not allowed to show that. It's wonderful to see him back, so all we want now is for him to be given a fair crack.'

A mere 68 seconds after the kick-off, Eric had the crowd on their feet. A pass from Cole found the Frenchman out on the left. It was his third touch of the game already, and he moved purposefully towards the Liverpool penalty area. At exactly the right moment, he released the ball in a curving cross which found Nicky Butt. Juggling the ball for a moment, Butt then guided it past David James and into the net. Pandemonium broke out. United's fans could not have dared hope for a better start.

Not that they had it all their own way. Liverpool then proceeded to take the match by the scruff of the neck, Robbie Fowler scoring twice. There were 20 minutes to go when Eric brought the house down again. Drawing defenders towards him, he slid the ball for Ryan Giggs to run on to in the penalty area. Seconds later Giggs had been sent sprawling by Jamie Redknapp, and the referee pointed to the spot. With the same confidence and self-belief that he had shown in the 1994 FA Cup final against Chelsea, Eric strode forward and stroked the penalty into the left-hand corner of the net.

It was a moment of magic. The crowd's celebrations drowned out the loudspeaker's announcement of the goal-scorer. As if anyone didn't know. In delight, Eric swung off the pole holding up the net behind the Liverpool goal – and then disappeared into the crowd. Only this time it wasn't in anger, but to receive the hugs and handshakes of United's cheering supporters. Watching in the stand were his parents and brothers, one of whom, Joel, exclaimed: 'It was an incredibly emotional day. When United got the penalty we were very nervous, but we had no fear. My father was excited, but he knew Eric would score because he is fearless in those situations.'

Not even Eric, though, could pull off the rescue mission that United required in the second leg of their Coca-Cola Cup tie with York. While they won 3–1 in Yorkshire, the result meant that the Second Division giant-killers went through 4–3 on aggregate. For his next run-out, in the reserves against Leeds to improve his match fitness, Eric was watched by 21,502 fans at Old Trafford – an attendance almost unheard of for a second eleven game. Worryingly, he picked up a knock and had to leave the field after only 18 minutes.

He was back in time for what was his first visit to

London since *that* night. The United squad arrived at Chelsea's Stamford Bridge ground surrounded by an army of security guards, causing one supporter to comment: 'Hold on, he attacked us.' Fortunately, the afternoon passed without incident, and Eric's cheeky flick set up Paul Scholes for the first of his two goals in a 4–1 victory. Mark Hughes, who scored Chelsea's solitary reply, said of his old team-mate: 'You can see he is getting back into his stride. He was very influential.'

What was also increasingly apparent was Eric's determination not to be ruffled. Southampton goalkeeper, Dave Beasant, went so far as to claim: 'I don't think he is a problem player at all now, just a great talent. You can see the change in Cantona. These days he doesn't get involved. I have watched him closely today and when he has been kicked by our players, he has just accepted it and talked to them. Rather than react, he has got up and got on with it.' This was a particularly charitable comment on Beasant's part, as United – prompted by Eric's sure touch and deadly passing – had just rattled four goals past him in another Premiership win.

Ferguson had also noted the change in Eric's attitude. 'He's always been a quiet person and he's still quiet, but what's happened to him has been the kind of experience that can't help but have an effect on your life. They say even a bad experience can be good for you, and maybe some good has come out of it,' the manager said. 'Since he came back into the team there have been refereeing decisions that he hasn't agreed with, but he's chosen not to argue. I've seen him walk quietly away from incidents that might have drawn a different reaction before.'

By the time the first anniversary of the Selhurst Park incident came round, Eric had even turned peacemaker on the pitch, pulling Andy Cole away from a furious confrontation with the referee in a match against West Ham, which could easily have ended with him being sent off. Instead, Eric calmed the situation down, and scored the winner for good measure. No wonder that Inter Milan were still trying to sign the Frenchman to play alongside Paul Ince, causing Ferguson to insist: 'He's going nowhere, and that's final.'

In the mean time, however, Newcastle seemed to have run away with the Premiership. By Christmas 1995, the Geordies were ten points clear of United. The two teams met at Old Trafford on 27 December and United cut back the gap at the top with a 2–0 victory. With Bruce injured, Eric captained the team and won the 'battle of the Frenchmen' which the media had eagerly forecast, by outplaying Newcastle's new signing, David Ginola. The win allowed Ferguson to celebrate his fifty-fourth birthday on New Year's Eve feeling a little more comfortable.

Not for long. Within three weeks, Newcastle had raced into a 12-point lead and looked unstoppable. United had even slipped into third place, behind Liverpool on goal difference. They had also just scraped through the FA Cup third round against Sunderland of the First Division after a replay. Had it not been for Eric's late equalizer, they would have lost the tie at Old Trafford. Ferguson hit back at the growing number of doubters. 'Some people seem to think the Cup is our more realistic hope of winning something this season. I disagree. I still think we have a real chance of winning the Premiership. That is in my sights, as well as another Wembley.' Steve Bruce backed him up: 'We are in the Cup and still in the title chase – and we're going for both. There is no way we are going to give up on the Double.'

Whether or not Bruce's words were just brave talk to rouse the team, they proved to be an accurate prediction. From the end of January 1996 onwards, they staged the most remarkable fightback, inspired above all by an astonishing sequence of goals from the man who had become the heartbeat of Manchester United. In spite of repeated attempts to provoke him (in one FA Cup tie at Reading a banana was hurled, and a coin hit a linesman, gashing him above the eye) Eric maintained his cool, picking up only one booking all season, while his habit of scoring when it mattered became uncanny.

Even his return to Selhurst Park, almost exactly a year after he had left the ground in shame, went without a hitch. In fact, it was a triumph. Eric scored twice as United beat Wimbledon 4–2, again watched by his father, who was the guest of honour of the London club's chairman, Sam Hamnam, in a kind gesture. In little more than a month, Newcastle's lead had been cut to four points, and United celebrated by smashing six past Bolton Wanderers away from home. The next match on their travels was the one which could decide the destination of the Premiership trophy: at St James's Park.

For the first 45 minutes United clung on in the face of a black and white hurricane which threatened to engulf them. Wave after wave of Newcastle attacks were pushed back, as Schmeichel's goal came under siege. Belgian international Philippe Albert almost broke United's crossbar with one free kick, and Colombian star Faustino Asprilla, making his home début, delighted Newcastle's fans with his trickery. But, at half-time, it was still 0–0. Six minutes later, Eric struck.

In one of United's rare moves upfield, Phil Neville fired in a dangerous-looking cross. The Frenchman came roaring into the penalty area to meet the ball, which he crashed past Pavel Srnicek in goal. The Newcastle fans could scarcely believe their eyes. The Newcastle players never got over it. United were now a single point behind. A week later they were through to the FA Cup semi-finals as well, beating Southampton 2–0 for their tenth win in a row. Yet again, Eric scored. Yet again, he was instrumental in setting up Lee Sharpe for the other goal.

So the pattern continued: an injury-time header to snatch a 1–1 draw at QPR; a 23-metre dipping volley to dispose of Arsenal 1–0; a fierce drive against Tottenham at Old Trafford in another 1–0 win; a penalty and the crucial pass to help Giggs score the winner in the 3–2 derby victory over Manchester City; the only goal of the game in the defeat of Coventry City – Eric's seventh in eight games. While no one, least of all Eric, was suggesting that this was a single-handed effort to capture the Double again, there was no argument about United's most vital player – as despairing opponents were the first to point out.

The turning-point came at Easter, as Newcastle suffered a heart-breaking late defeat at Blackburn after taking the lead, following soon after an epic match at Anfield, which they had also lost to Liverpool 4–3. United were on top of the table again, and except for one hiccup – a 3–1 defeat at Southampton which the players bizarrely blamed on not being able to see each other properly in their grey away strip – they were not to be knocked off their perch again. They were already at Wembley, having overcome Chelsea 2–1 in the semi-final after going behind to a Ruud Gullit goal.

The tension surrounding the last few games of the Premiership was enormous, at one point leading to a heated row between Ferguson and Newcastle boss Keegan. But Newcastle let their best remaining chance slip away in the final week of the season, when they failed to win at Nottingham Forest after taking the lead. United's last match was a visit to Middlesbrough, whose manager was Old Trafford's former favourite, Bryan Robson. Newcastle needed to win at Tottenham, and hope that United lost.

There was never really any prospect of that happening. David May, Andy Cole and Ryan Giggs clinched United's third Premiership in four seasons with their goals, as Newcastle could manage only a draw in London. Eric's amazing contribution to that achievement had already been recognized by the journalists of the Football Writers' Association, who named him Footballer of the Year, the 49th winner of the award, following in the footsteps of such previous giants as Sir Stanley Matthews and Bobby Moore. He was also fittingly the first Manchester United player to claim the honour since George Best in 1968.

Receiving the award, Eric said: 'I am very proud and privileged to have been voted Footballer of the Year. It is a tremendous honour for me and my country and it is a great tribute to my fellow players at Manchester United.' Alex Ferguson claimed: 'This award proves the value of British justice. It is well deserved because there is no doubt that Eric Cantona has been the best player in the country this season.'

That season there was one last stage on which Eric could again prove his manager's claim. Liverpool stood between United and a second Premiership and Cup Double, which no team had ever accomplished before. It was the first time that the two clubs had met in an FA Cup final since 1977 (when United had won 2–1) and all the talk before the game was of a spectacle to compare with any of the great finals.

In the event, it was a hugely disappointing game. Liverpool's performance, in particular, was a mere shadow of what they were capable of producing. Then, with so little time remaining, the ball came out from the scramble which followed the corner-kick, to the edge of the penalty area – and Eric.

If, as the ball landed in front of him, his mind wandered back to a day long ago when an undone bootlace and a referee's whistle had prevented him winning a previous team a league and cup double, he never showed it. This time, nothing was going to deny Eric – and Manchester United – his place in history.

CHAPTER SEVEN

King of Old Trafford

A S MANCHESTER UNITED RETURNED home from Wembley and the scene of their un-equalled second Double in three years, Sir Bobby Charlton paid the ultimate tribute to Eric Cantona, when he declared: 'This man is as great a player as any to have worn the red of Manchester United. I wouldn't swap him for any footballer in the world.'

Coming from such an Old Trafford legend as Sir Bobby, there could be no higher praise. But his words were echoed by everyone connected with the club. Alex Ferguson, who had recognized Eric's importance to the team before anyone else, joked that, with the Frenchman playing, his side could 'climb Everest in carpet slippers'. It is, probably more than anything else, that deep friendship between manager and player which is behind United's most recent success.

The two men share many similarities. In the dark-est days, when Eric was at his lowest after running into trouble with the football authorities again, it was Ferguson who lifted him. 'I stressed to Eric the need to control himself or he would lose everything,' he recalled later. 'At the same time I told him I knew what it was like because as a player I was sent off five or six times in my career. As soon as I told him that he smiled and I think he looked at me in a new light, someone who had been through a similar battle with temperament, a kindred spirit if you like. I think we understood one another better.'

Likewise, Eric never forgot the chance that Ferguson gave him after the Selhurst Park incident. 'The greatest emotion I felt came a short time after the Crystal Palace affair. I was banished and down, and nobody wanted to hear about me, but Alex Ferguson and the other club leaders redrew my contract for two years, raised my pay and gave me additional match bonuses. I never would have believed I would be treated so well when I was in such a deep hole. I owe these people so much because they have behaved with such elegance.'

The fact that he did stay at United also has a lot to do with Sir Bobby. In the aftermath of his attack on the fan at Crystal Palace, it was the former Old Trafford star who took him to one side. 'When I was in the depth of the storm, it was Bobby Charlton who talked to me about the future. He had decided to help me look ahead. Where else but at Manchester United could I have received that?' he told *Paris Match* magazine. 'Manchester United is the club where I have experienced the greatest emotion of my playing career. When I came back against Liverpool after eight months, it was extraordinary, with French flags everywhere and people singing.'

His enormous value to United goes beyond what he does on the field of play. Some estimates suggest that he is worth £10 million to the club, because his name helps sell so many products, from posters and T-shirts, to mugs, hats, scarves, ties and even bedspreads. Eric's name is on a third of all the team shirts sold at the Manchester United Megastore at Old Trafford. His first video, *Eric the King*, sold more than 200,000 copies, to send it straight to the top in the video-selling charts. Sales of its follow-up, *The Return of the Magnificent Seven*, look set to more than equal that.

Strangely, Eric's popularity in England is not matched in his home country. In the French television version of *Spitting Image*, his puppet is called Picasso, spouts pretentious nonsense, and paints red cards which he then shows himself. Eric's early retirement from the game in France seems to have coloured the French's attitude towards him, and there was little sense of surprise across the Channel over the Selhurst Park controversy. 'Cantona's blown a circuit again' was how one French newsreader summed it up.

He has not played for the French national team since appearing in a friendly against Holland a week before that night and, at present, looks unlikely to do so again. The French manager, Aimé Jacquet, built up a young team, which enjoyed a long winning streak of 20 games in the build-up to the European Championships in England, without ever playing Eric or Newcastle's French import, David Ginola. Neither was named in France's squad for Euro '96.

Being left out of such a major tournament was a big blow to someone as proud as Eric. He has made little comment about his omission by Jacquet, except to say: 'I thought my 45 caps and 20 goals for France could have been taken into consideration.' The French football authorities were swamped by angry telephone calls and letters demanding Eric's inclusion after the squad was announced. But Jacquet made no apology about his decision. 'I have no qualms about my choice,' he said. 'I have weighed up the merits of all the best French players, including Cantona. Besides, I have no duty to British crowds.' Unless France has a change of heart – or a change of manager – Eric could also miss out on the biggest stage of all: the 1998 World Cup, which is being hosted by the French.

However, his chances of appearing in the greatest football show on earth have not entirely disappeared. Although France reached the semi-finals of Euro '96, they had to rely on a penalty shoot-out to get them through the quarter-final against Holland after a boring 0–0 draw, and they were then knocked out on penalties by the Czech Republic, at Old Trafford, after another goalless stalemate. The leading French newspaper, *France Soir*, reported afterwards: 'The shadow of Eric Cantona hung over Old Trafford. Cantona was axed by Jacquet for fear that his overwhelming personality might hamper France's solidarity. Cantona disturbs. He is a troublemaker, but he scores goals.' If serious doubts grow about France's ability to win the World Cup on their own territory, then a recall for Eric must be on the cards.

While the manager of France does not appear to have the highest regard for Eric, the new manager of England is one of his biggest admirers. Glenn Hoddle, who recommended the Frenchman to a number of clubs when he first arrived in this country, believes that Eric is an excellent influence on the youngsters around him at Old Trafford. 'Manchester United have a great crop of young players who are being brought on by the example of Cantona,' he claimed.

In the 1996/97 season, he will be leading those players into the European Cup, the competition that United want to win most of all. At 30 years old, Eric is at the peak of his playing powers, and he believes that the team he is in at the moment is the one which can finally bring home the only trophy to escape Alex Ferguson's grasp. 'Next season is very important. We're trying for the Double – the European Cup and the Premiership. Our young players are very good tactically and technically. We are like a European team and must have a very good chance in Europe. I'm happy I stayed. It's a great club. It can win everything.'

Giving interviews is something of a rarity for Eric, who did not speak publicly for 15 months after his court appearance. Incidentally, the spectator, Matthew Simmons, was found guilty of using threatening words and behaviour, fined £500, and banned from football grounds for a year. Then, incredibly, he attacked the prosecuting lawyer, for which he was given a seven-day jail sentence, serving only one night before being released. On one occasion, Eric famously told reporters: 'When seagulls follow a trawler, it is because they think sardines will be thrown into the sea.' Much of the press treated his comment as a joke, and pretended they could not understand what he was talking about. But his meaning – that reporters followed him around, waiting for him to do something that would make a story – was perfectly plain.

However, on the eve of the FA Cup final, he told Desmond Lynam in a BBC1 interview that he would be staying at United and may even remain in the game after his retirement. He said he intended to be around for 'two more years, maybe longer'. But perhaps the most surprising hint about his future came when he revealed: 'I may be a manager here in England.'

Certainly, given his loyalty to the club, and the fans' strength of feeling for their French hero, it seems unlikely that Eric Cantona will play for anyone else but Manchester United. As the leader of a young team which is shaping up to be one of the greatest yet to play in the red shirts, he has a glorious opportunity to be the captain of a European Cup-winning squad, a fitting pinnacle for his career. And if he was eventually to succeed Alex Ferguson in the manager's seat at Old Trafford, there would be no more popular choice among the club's army of supporters around the world.

The
UFO
Investigator's
Handbook

by Marc Gascoigne

The truth is in here . . .

UFOs, extra-terrestrials or just white lights and hoaxers – depending on who you believe, the world is either under constant threat from alien invasion or it is simply full of weirdos. But what is the truth? You can decide for yourself in this amazing book.

* The early sightings – Foo fighters and airship scares
* Close encounters – the famous stories
* The Roswell incident – superbeing or plastic dummy?

Look at the facts, seek out the truth. Before you know it, you'll be investigating your very own *X-Files*™.

READ MORE IN PUFFIN

For children of all ages, Puffin represents quality and variety – the very best in publishing today around the world.

For complete information about books available from Puffin – and Penguin – and how to order them, contact us at the appropriate address below. Please note that for copyright reasons the selection of books varies from country to country.

On the world wide web: www.penguin.co.uk

In the United Kingdom: Please write to *Dept. EP, Penguin Books Ltd, Bath Road, Harmondsworth, West Drayton, Middlesex UB7 ODA*

In the United States: Please write to *Consumer Sales, Penguin USA, P.O. Box 999, Dept. 17109, Bergenfield, New Jersey 07621-0120.* VISA and MasterCard holders call 1-800-253-6476 to order Penguin titles

In Canada: Please write to *Penguin Books Canada Ltd, 10 Alcorn Avenue, Suite 300, Toronto, Ontario M4V 3B2*

In Australia: Please write to *Penguin Books Australia Ltd, P.O. Box 257, Ringwood, Victoria 3134*

In New Zealand: Please write to *Penguin Books (NZ) Ltd, Private Bag 102902, North Shore Mail Centre, Auckland 10*

In India: Please write to *Penguin Books India Pvt Ltd, 706 Eros Apartments, 56 Nehru Place, New Delhi 110 019*

In the Netherlands: Please write to *Penguin Books Netherlands bv, Postbus 3507, NL-1001 AH Amsterdam*

In Germany: Please write to *Penguin Books Deutschland GmbH, Metzlerstrasse 26, 60594 Frankfurt am Main*

In Spain: Please write to *Penguin Books S. A., Bravo Murillo 19, 1° B, 28015 Madrid*

In Italy: Please write to *Penguin Italia s.r.l., Via Felice Casati 20, I–20124 Milano*

In France: Please write to *Penguin France S. A., 17 rue Lejeune, F–31000 Toulouse*

In Japan: Please write to *Penguin Books Japan, Ishikiribashi Building, 2–5–4, Suido, Bunkyo-ku, Tokyo 112*

In South Africa: Please write to *Longman Penguin Southern Africa (Pty) Ltd, Private Bag X08, Bertsham 2013*